T0233353

Developing Conversational Interfaces for iOS

Add Responsive Voice Control to Your Apps

Martin Mitrevski

Apress®

Developing Conversational Interfaces for iOS: Add Responsive Voice Control to Your Apps

Martin Mitrevski
Ohrid, Macedonia

ISBN-13 (pbk): 978-1-4842-3395-5   ISBN-13 (electronic): 978-1-4842-3396-2
https://doi.org/10.1007/978-1-4842-3396-2

Library of Congress Control Number: 2017964661

Cover image designed by Freepik.

Managing Director: Welmoed Spahr
Editorial Director: Todd Green
Acquisitions Editor: Aaron Black
Development Editor: James Markham
Technical Reviewer: Felipe Laso-Marsetti
Coordinating Editor: Jessica Vakili
Copy Editor: Kim Wimpsett
Compositor: SPi Global
Indexer: SPi Global
Artist: SPi Global

Distributed to the book trade worldwide by Springer Science+Business Media New York, 233 Spring Street, 6th Floor, New York, NY 10013. Phone 1-800-SPRINGER, fax (201) 348-4505, e-mail orders-ny@springer-sbm.com, or visit www.springeronline.com. Apress Media, LLC is a California LLC and the sole member (owner) is Springer Science + Business Media Finance Inc (SSBM Finance Inc). SSBM Finance Inc is a **Delaware** corporation.

For information on translations, please e-mail rights@apress.com, or visit www.apress.com/rights-permissions.

Apress titles may be purchased in bulk for academic, corporate, or promotional use. eBook versions and licenses are also available for most titles. For more information, reference our Print and eBook Bulk Sales web page at www.apress.com/bulk-sales.

Any source code or other supplementary material referenced by the author in this book is available to readers on GitHub via the book's product page, located at www.apress.com/978-1-4842-3395-5. For more detailed information, please visit www.apress.com/source-code.

Printed on acid-free paper

To my family: my parents, Lidija and Dimche;
my brother, Viktor, and his wife, Emma;
and my beautiful girlfriend, Natasha.

Thanks for all the support and patience!

Table of Contents

About the Author

Martin Mitrevski is currently a senior software engineer and tech lead at Netcetera. He's developed mobile apps in the areas of virtual reality, transport, indoor navigation, publishing, insurance, weather, innovation tools, and live event apps.

Martin is enthusiastic about technology, well-crafted code, books, innovation, and everything that leads us to new and better directions. He likes to follow the latest mobile trends and software development principles in general.

Lately, he's been fascinated by the possibilities that conversational interfaces bring in simplifying the user experience and how they might change the way we think about apps. Martin is always happy to exchange knowledge with others on his blog at `https://martinmitrevski.com` and as a conference speaker. You can follow him on Twitter via the handle `@mitrevski`.

About the Technical Reviewer

Felipe Laso-Marsetti is a senior systems engineer working at Lextech Global Services. He's also an aspiring game designer/programmer. You can follow him on Twitter via @iFeliLM or on his blog at http://ifeli.me/.

Introduction

User interfaces in mobile apps are continuing to evolve by recognizing the most natural way for users to express their wishes: their voice.

Conversational interfaces are starting to get a lot of attention, mostly because of the latest advancements in natural language understanding and machine learning.

All the big players provide tools and voice assistants in this area. Apple has Siri and the Speech framework, Google has Google Assistant and Dialogflow, Amazon has Alexa and Lex, and Microsoft has Cortana and LUIS. This topic is exciting and will be even more so in the future.

Currently, there's no book on the market that incorporates all aspects of conversational interfaces on iOS, starting from voice transcription, natural language processing, intent detection, and entities extraction and going all the way to text-to-speech commands.

The book will help you build conversationally aware and smarter iOS applications. With the introduction of the new platforms and exciting technologies, iOS developers now have huge opportunities to take their apps to the next level. In this book, you will be familiarized with the following topics:

- Apple's SiriKit framework

- Apple's Speech framework

- Google's Dialogflow language-understanding platform

- Facebook's Wit.ai language-understanding platform

- The basics of natural language processing on iOS

- Sentiment analysis with Apple's new Core ML framework

- The challenges of conversational interfaces and what the future brings

Who This Book is For

The primary audience for the book includes iOS developers, product and innovation managers, and potentially UX experts. It will be helpful to all engineers and managers who want to provide conversational interfaces in their apps.

This book does not cover the basics of iOS development. Specifically, it will not show the steps to create a new Xcode project or introduce you to basic iOS development concepts. Having that knowledge is a prerequisite for getting the most from the book.

What You'll Need

To follow along and run the code examples in this book, you will need a Mac with macOS Sierra, 10.12.6 or higher. You will also need to have Xcode 9 or higher, with Swift 4.

CHAPTER 1

Conversational Interfaces

People and computers speak different languages—people use words and sentences, while computers are more into ones and zeros. This gap in communication is filled with a mediator that knows how to translate all the information flowing between the two parts. These mediators are called *graphical user interfaces* (GUIs).

GUI Beginnings

Historically, there have been three major breakthroughs in the quest to create the most suitable user interfaces. The first one was in Xerox's research lab, where Steve Jobs recognized the huge potential of the mouse cursor clicking around a desktop, opening folders, copying and pasting files, and much more (Figure 1-1). It was a revolutionary approach that made computers accessible to a much broader audience, and it's still used today.

© Martin Mitrevski 2018
M. Mitrevski, *Developing Conversational Interfaces for iOS*,
https://doi.org/10.1007/978-1-4842-3396-2_1

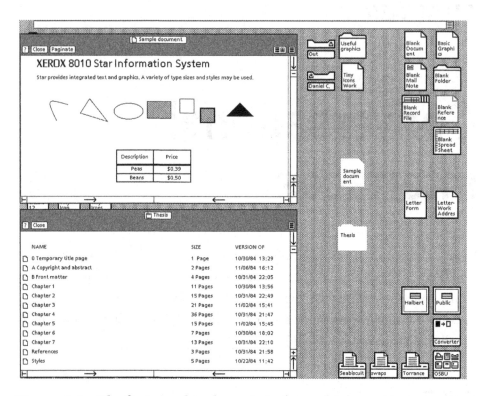

Figure 1-1. *The first graphical user interface*

The second revolution was also something Steve Jobs managed to introduce on a massive scale.

> *"We're gonna use the best pointing device in the world. We're gonna use a pointing device that we're all born with—we're born with ten of them. We're gonna use our fingers."*

These Steve Jobs words about the iPhone's unveiling introduced the multitouch concept, which is now widely used on all mobile devices. It was another natural but revolutionary step in providing the most intuitive experience for users (Figure 1-2).

Figure 1-2. *The iPhone's multitouch user interface*

These two approaches made interaction with machines (whether that be computers or mobile devices) much easier and accessible.

The third major breakthrough is what this book is all about: conversational interfaces. Before I get to that, let's take a moment to talk about GUI challenges.

Graphical User Interfaces Challenges

One commonality between these GUIs is that people need to learn how to interact with them. For example, they need to know that a single click on a folder will select that folder and that a double-click will open it. They need to know there's a "back" hardware button on Android phones but a similar software button (styled differently) in every iOS application. Having many

3

different options and different implementations of the two concepts can be confusing for the users. Everyone who has switched from a Windows to a Mac (or vice versa) knows that you need few days (or even weeks) to learn how to efficiently use the different operating system. The same applies to phones—although they all follow the multitouch concept, the transition from one OS to another can take some time.

Another challenge that current GUIs face is the new set of devices recently introduced to the market—wearables. When you have a screen as small as a watch, clicking it to perform some task can be quite a tedious experience. And these devices are targeted mostly to modern, on-the-go users who need some information fast with minimal fuss.

This brings the need for a completely different user interface—one that will unify all the different platforms and will perform tasks for users with little interaction. And what's the most natural way of expressing your needs? Of course, it's by using your voice to create words and sentences.

Voice as a User Interface

So, the third major breakthrough in user interfaces is a nongraphical one: conversational interfaces. The idea is not new. We've seen it in a lot of movies, usually in the form of some virtual assistant that informs the main character of some new danger ahead. Or the character falls in love with his assistant (like in the 2013 movie *Her*). Generally speaking, movies can be an interesting source of inspiration for the next innovations in technology. Hollywood is a place where technology meets the liberal arts, and it can have a big impact on consumer technology. Did you know the interactive newspapers in *Harry Potter* inspired Facebook to introduce self-starting videos in its news feeds? Or that the gesture-driven UI in *Minority Report* is what now you basically do in interacting with your mobile device? Keep that in mind: inspiration can come from unexpected places.

Understanding Language

Since the idea for conversational interfaces is not that new, why did it take so long for the big tech companies to start making products with them? The main reason is that speech recognition and natural language understanding are two of the most challenging problems in computer science. Sometimes even one small word (such as *not*, for example) can completely change the meaning of a sentence. Also, punctuation can introduce different meanings to words. Computers are not like humans; they don't talk with each other in a free-form manner all the time, learning new phrases and meanings along the way. They are pretty exact entities, and they do what they are told to do.

Language is the primary form of communication between humans. It is used to express everything from our feelings to explanations of how we have solved complex programming tasks. This wide range of phrases, expressions, and wishes is dependent on many other circumstances, such as the context in which the phrase is spoken, the beliefs of the people involved in the conversation, and suggestions that are not directly implied by the phrase (called *implicatures*). For example, say you ask a person who lives with you "Where is my football T-shirt?" and they reply "Can't you hear the washing machine working?" You can infer that the T-shirt is currently being laundered in the washing machine. Adding to the complexity of the language are *presuppositions*, which are implicit assumptions about something related to a phrase that's taken for granted as being true. For example, if you say "I haven't coded for two years," the presupposition is that you once coded. The same presupposition holds, even if you say "I have coded for two years."

There are cases where understanding language can be difficult for humans as well. Sometimes you might run into words that are unknown to you and you must guess what they mean. Or even when you understand the words, the meaning can be ambiguous; in other words, you are not sure what the speaker intended to say. If someone says "Did you see her dress?" that might mean many different things. It can mean that a girl can't find her dress and someone is asking around for help. It can also be interpreted as someone checking on whether she has started dressing. Or it can be a gossip between people about the way the girl is dressed.

Figurative speech is another challenge. Using metaphors, similes, and allusions that go beyond the literal meaning of words gives a sentence a whole new meaning. Extracting the correct meaning is a demanding task for humans, so you can imagine how difficult it would be for a computer.

However, artificial intelligence, machine learning, and natural language processing have been making some impressive improvements in the past few years. Engineers are developing sophisticated deep learning algorithms and feeding them with massive amounts of data. Providing as many examples and training sets as possible makes it easier for computers to figure out what users are saying.

Products on the Market

These technological advancements have triggered the creation of new products from every major tech company in this area. Apple has Siri, which is now open for iOS developers through the SiriKit framework. Developers can handle voice commands in their apps that users give to Siri. For example, imagine a user rushing to find a ride to the airport. They will say something like, "Hey, Siri, book me a ride to the airport using YourCoolApp." Siri will ask your app whether it can handle the request, and the app might ask for some additional information, such as where you want to be picked up (or maybe it would just use the user's current location) or what type of ride you want (car, taxi, train, etc.). Then Siri presents the information from your app inside Siri (your app is not opened; everything happens in Siri's context), and if the user agrees to the provided ride offer, your app then reserves the ride, and Siri notifies the user about the status.

Google has OK Google and Google Assistant, which support similar functionalities and extension points for developers. One interesting product from Google is Dialogflow (formerly api.ai), which is a web application through which developers can train the platform to learn how to recognize and extract parts of the sentences and return them in JSON format. This gives developers more flexibility and releases the burden from them in terms of developing complex natural language processing (NLP) solutions by themselves. NLP is a field in artificial intelligence that tries to analyze and understand the meaning of human language.

Facebook's Wit.ai is another platform that provides excellent tools for developers to add conversational interfaces to their apps. Microsoft has LUIS, a web application through which you can train how the platform recognizes entities in a sentence. In addition, Microsoft has Cortana, its virtual assistant named after a character in the video game *Halo*. Amazon provides Alexa Skill Set and Amazon Lex. With Amazon Lex, the same natural-understanding platform that is used by Amazon Alexa is available to developers. If you need a reliable enterprise solution, IBM has Watson, with several products that support easier creation of virtual agents and chatbots with a specific domain business knowledge.

Overview of the Process

Let's look at the products and technologies from the viewpoint of a developer. Integrating a technology that provides a conversational interface to your application requires several steps. These steps might be already integrated in the product. They can also be partially integrated, providing you with customization points that you can use to provide domain-specific knowledge, use a different technology for that customization point, or even provide your own implementation. Figure 1-3 shows an outline of how to add a conversational interface to your iOS application.

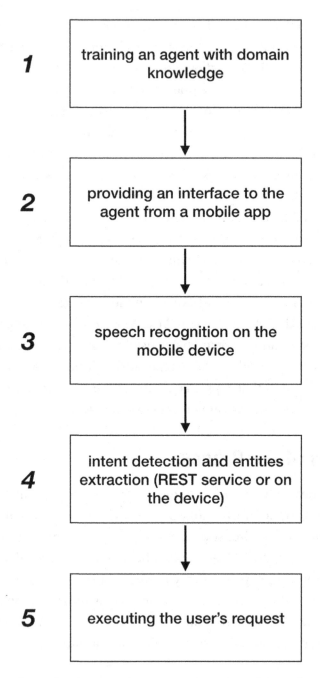

Figure 1-3. *Steps for integrating a conversational interface product*

The first step is to build an agent with the domain-specific knowledge. Building the agent requires infrastructure (data storage, servers), natural language–understanding algorithms, and the actual training with the business domain knowledge. The provider of the agent has to make the service available to the mobile devices in some way—either as a REST service or as a native framework.

Next, the mobile device has to convert the user's spoken phrase to a machine-readable string. This is usually done on the device, although an external REST service might also be used. After the string is detected, it is sent to the trained agent, which tries to extract the user's intent and the parameters of that intent (entities) based on the training that was provided in the first step. If the intent and the entities are extracted successfully, the app has enough information to execute the user's request and provide results of the action.

What the Products Do

Based on the previous overview, let's see what the current products on the market provide in terms of integrating conversational interfaces in a mobile application. Table 1-1 illustrates the differences between them.

Table 1-1. *Conversational Interface Products That Can Be Integrated into iOS Apps*

Product	Infrastructure	Speech Recognition	Training	Natural language understanding
SiriKit	Provided	Provided	Provided	Provided
Dialogflow	Provided	Not provided	Both options	Provided
Wit.ai	Provided	Provided	Both options	Provided
Amazon LEX	Provided	Provided	Both options	Provided
LUIS	Provided	Not provided	Both options	Provided
Core ML	Not provided	Not provided	Not provided	Not provided

First I'll define what the values in this table mean. The "Provided" value indicates that the service is already enabled (implemented) in the product and you don't need to do anything by yourself. The "Not provided" value means the service is not available in the product and you need to use other products to fill this gap or implement it by yourself. The "Both options" value indicates that the product provides both a predefined solution for the particular service and a customization point if the developers want to provide app-specific functionality.

SiriKit does all the heavy lifting for you when integrating conversational interfaces to your app. The testing data and the algorithms are stored and running on Apple's infrastructure. The speech recognition is done by the framework itself, which also does the training and the natural language understanding. You, as a developer, just receive callbacks with values for predefined intents and entities. That doesn't leave much room for customization. If the currently supported domains are not fitting your application's goal, then you can't make much use of the framework. You will get to know SiriKit in more detail in Chapters 2 and 3.

Dialogflow, Wit.ai, Amazon LEX, and LUIS are similar services that provide you with infrastructure and the possibility to train your own agents. Those agents are available to mobile apps as a REST service. In addition to the ability to train your own models, they provide already trained agents, which can be directly used for common things such as checking the weather, setting an alarm, booking a ride or flight, and more.

Some of the products, such as Wit.ai and Amazon LEX, provide iOS SDKs that do the speech recognition part on the mobile device. Others, such as Dialogflow and LUIS, still don't have such support, which means you have to use other frameworks, such as Apple's Speech, that convert the user's spoken input to text. You can find more details on Dialogflow and Wit.ai in Chapters 4 and 5.

You can take a different approach as well, with Apple's Core ML framework for machine learning. With this approach, you are in charge of finding or creating the dataset, implementing the machine learning algorithm, and training and testing the agent. Apple just provides the glue that enables easier integration of the model in an iOS application. You will explore Core ML in Chapter 7.

Conversational Interfaces Flow

You have probably seen the YouTube video where a kid asks Alexa to play him something like "tickle, tickle" and Alexa responds with some adult movie suggestions.

These comical situations are not rare since there's still a lot of room for improvement in this area. Users have to be as concise as possible and have to find the right structure of sentences that virtual assistants will understand. To address this broad range of different sentences, the frameworks are offering a bit restrictive flow—they have a few predefined domains (use cases), which are triggered by already defined sentences. They encourage you to avoid open questions and to provide users with different options. For example, if a user wants a train ride from London to Paris, Siri can ask the user "What type of ride do you want?" and your app can provide a few options that Siri will relay to the user, such as first-class or second-class ticket. Also, the SDKs are designed in a way that you need to find the user's preferences by asking one question at a time and then proceed with the next question only after you have the answer of the current one. For example, after you know the type of the ride, Siri might next ask the user "Where do you want to go?" if they didn't specify that in the voice command. Notice also that the questions are pretty simple and clear and they ask for only one piece of information.

This new way of interacting with users is a challenge for developers and user experience experts. There are still no common best practices; you need to experiment and figure out what works and what doesn't. In any case, the future is exciting, and you will see a lot more innovation in this area.

Natural Language–Understanding Concepts

So that you can understand the examples in the next few chapters, in this section I will cover the concepts that are important for natural language-processing engineering.

The most important concept in conversational interfaces is an *intent*. This is basically what the user wants the system (application or chatbot) to do. The system might provide several intents. For example, a grocery list application might provide intents for adding, removing, and marking products as bought. It might also provide the ability to directly pay for the products in a list or send the bill to someone else to pay. The first step in natural language processing is to figure out which of the intents you have provided matches the spoken phrase of the user.

There might be cases where there is no mapping of the user input to a specific action. This can happen if the user asks for something you can't provide. For example, they might ask "Deliver the products of the grocery list to my address," but your system doesn't provide such an intent. No matching can also happen if the model you train with sentences is not complete. For example, the user might say "Get rid of milk from my list," which clearly means the user wants to remove milk from their list. But if you haven't provided sentences similar to this one, your model might not recognize the user's intent. Training the model with the domain knowledge specific to the functionality the system provides and with as many sentences as possible is one of the most challenging tasks in natural language processing. That is what gives the system the ability to react to lots of different natural spoken phrases.

After the intent is recognized, you need to figure out what are the *parameters* of that action. These are also called *entities*. In the grocery list example, if you have figured out that the user's intent is to add products to the list, the next step is to determine what those products are. In this case, the entities belong to the defined type of products. There are some common entities to most intents, such as location, date, time, temperature, and many more.

What's interesting is that entities can appear multiple times in intents but with different meanings. For example, a location entity appears twice in a "booking a ride" intent. If the user says "I want a ride from Paris to London," the first location entity represents the pickup location of the user, and the second one represents the user's destination. In the process of training the model, this can be accomplished by defining two (or more) different roles of the same entity and marking the entity and its role in the sentence in as many examples as possible.

Another challenge here is that even if you need two entities from one intent to execute the user's request, the user might provide only one. They might have forgotten that you need the other value, or they might expect this to be inferred. In the "booking a ride" example, they might expect that you take their pickup location from the location services on the device. However, if for various reasons you are not able to get the needed values from the first input, you should ask the user for the specific value you are missing. Asking the user to say the full sentence again with the missing information is not a good user experience.

Usually in conversational interface systems, the user will ask several things during the conversation. It is expected that the system stores the information about the previous data the user has provided. Storing the parameters from previous expressions is usually called *context*. For example, you are ordering a sandwich from a chatbot and give information about whether the sandwich should contain ham, cheese, ketchup, olives, and so on. Then, if you want to order another one just like the previous one but without olives, you should be able to say this in a natural manner: "Same as previous one but without olives." Using context, you can accomplish this. During one conversation, there might be several contexts. The whole conversation, from start to end, is usually called a *session*.

Figure 1-4 shows the process of food ordering with a chatbot. The user provides a sentence in a plain-text or spoken phrase. The text is processed, and an intent is detected, along with the entities of the intent. After that, the user specifies another request connected with the previous state (sandwich ordering), and the chatbot detects from the context which previous information is required to complete this request. Then, the chatbot asks the user about a drink, thus triggering a different context. The user might later say, for example, "without ice" or "another one to go." These multiple contexts represent one session, which is the whole interaction between the user and the chatbot during the ordering experience.

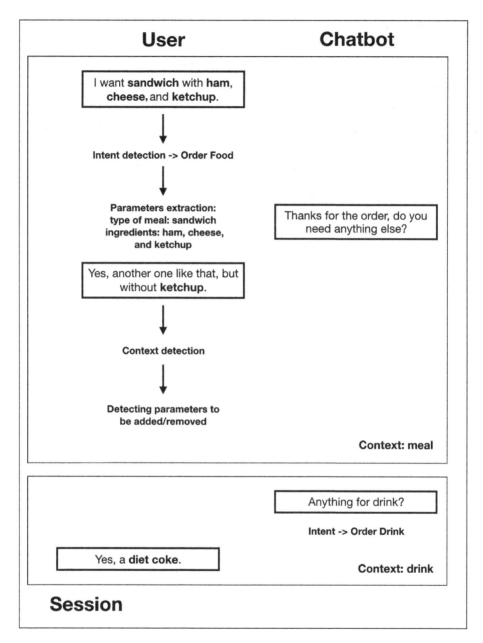

Figure 1-4. *Food ordering interaction with a chatbot*

Summary

As you've seen, finding an appropriate GUI can be quite a challenge—and it's basically the key factor in determining whether your software will be used. If users don't understand the interactions they need to do to get the most out of it, they will not use it. That's why the GUIs must be intuitive and easy to learn.

In the following chapters, you will see practical applications of these natural language–understanding concepts in iOS projects. You will start with Apple's SiriKit framework in the next two chapters by building two apps, one for booking a ride and the other one for adding and removing items in a grocery list.

CHAPTER 2

Booking a Ride with SiriKit

At the WWDC conference in 2016, Apple announced SiriKit, which enables developers to provide functionality that can be executed directly from Siri, without opening the main application. This is another step to the idea of using new, innovative ways to interact with users via conversational interfaces, simplifying the whole user experience. Your app can now provide functionality to Siri directly from the lock screen and when the app is not even started. However, as is usually the case with Apple, there are some limitations. You can use SiriKit only for certain predefined domains.

- VoIP calling

- Messaging

- Payments

- Lists and Notes

- Visual Codes

- Photos

- Workouts

- Ride booking

© Martin Mitrevski 2018
M. Mitrevski, *Developing Conversational Interfaces for iOS*,
https://doi.org/10.1007/978-1-4842-3396-2_2

- Car Commands/CarPlay

- Restaurant reservations

What do these domains mean, and what can they do for you as a user? You can, for example, send messages and make calls directly from Siri. You can send money to someone or check your account's status. You can create to-do lists and notes and add items to them. You can ask Siri to show you your football game ticket when you get near the stadium with the new Visual Codes extension. Siri can also show you photos or book you a ride. With the Car Commands extension, you can manage vehicle door locks and get a vehicle's status (handy for the people who are unsure whether they have locked their car's doors). And with SiriKit, you can make restaurant reservations with the help of the Maps application. Although it's a limited set of domains, SiriKit provides lots of possibilities for innovation and improving the user experience. Also, probably in the future more domains will be added, like when the Lists and Notes and Visual Codes extensions were added in iOS 11. If your app is not solving problems in one of those domains, you will need to wait for (or even suggest to Apple) an extension in the domain that your app needs.

Booking a Ride

In this chapter, you will look at the ride-booking domain. You will build a simple app that will reserve a (fake) ride between two locations provided by the user. Let's get started!

Before you develop a Siri extension, you need to build the mobile app, which will provide the base "booking a ride" functionality. The UI will be pretty simple; as shown in Figure 2-1, it contains just two text fields for the "from" and "to" locations, as well as a button that will start the booking. When the button is tapped, the found rides are displayed in a list below it. The user interface is already set up for you in the starter project for this chapter.

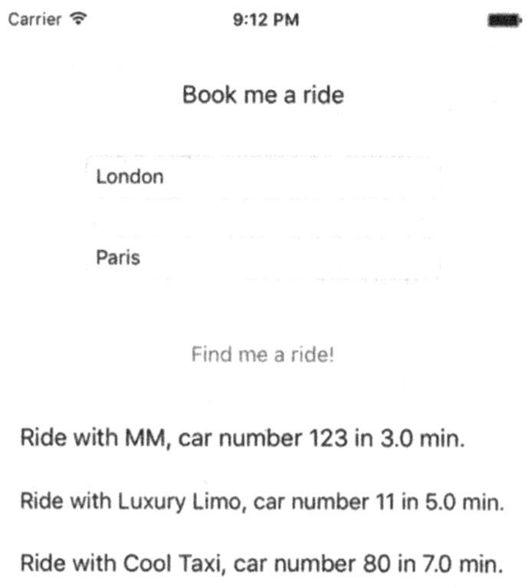

Carrier 🛜   9:12 PM   ▬▬▬

Book me a ride

London

Paris

Find me a ride!

Ride with MM, car number 123 in 3.0 min.

Ride with Luxury Limo, car number 11 in 5.0 min.

Ride with Cool Taxi, car number 80 in 7.0 min.

Figure 2-1. *Simple ride-booking app*

The scope of this chapter will be exploring the SiriKit functionalities, so you will not be connecting to a real ride-booking service. If you want to connect to such an API, depending on the country you want to support, there are few options, such as the Uber and Ola APIs. Instead, you will just create a list of dummy rides that you will offer to users. You will follow a *protocol-oriented* approach to replace the dummy service without many code changes. Let's start by creating a single-view application called BookMeARide (or open the starter project). Create a new Swift file called RideService.swift and define a protocol for finding rides (Listing 2-1).

Listing 2-1. RideService Protocol

```
protocol RideService {
    func findRide(from: String, to: String, completion:
    @escaping ([Ride]) -> Void)
}
```

Tip In general, protocols in Swift, combined with structs and other value types, are really powerful and have more benefits than using classes and inheritance, which is what you are used to in traditional object-oriented programming. Protocols provide flexibility, whereas class inheritance is too intrusive.

This method defines what you should expect from a ride-booking service—finding list of possible rides, depending on the starting and ending locations. The ride type will be a simple struct (Listing 2-2), which will contain basic ride information, such as the company, the car number, the expected time in minutes when the car can pick you up, the type of the ride (whether it's a limo or taxi), and, of course, how much it would cost the user. Here you use a struct over a class, because structs are lightweight, are cheap to create, and don't have the implicit sharing burden that comes with classes. Enter this code in a new file called Ride.swift.

Listing 2-2. RideType and Ride Types

```swift
enum RideType {
    case taxi
    case limo
}

struct Ride {
    var company: String
    var carNumber: String
    var timeInMinutes: Double
    var rideType: RideType
    var price: Float
    var currency: String
}
```

Next, create a dummy implementation of the RideService protocol in a file called DummyRideService.swift, which will return a few hard-coded rides (Listing 2-3).

Listing 2-3. Service Returning Hard-Coded Rides

```swift
class DummyRideService: NSObject, RideService {

    func findRide(from: String, to: String, completion:
    @escaping ([Ride]) -> Void) {
        completion(self.dummyRides())
    }

    private func dummyRides() -> [Ride] {
        let ride1 = Ride(company: "MM",
                        carNumber: "123",
                        timeInMinutes: 3,
                        rideType: .taxi,
                        price: 30,
                        currency: "EUR")

        let ride2 = Ride(company: "Luxury Limo",
                        carNumber: "11",
                        timeInMinutes: 5,
                        rideType: .limo,
                        price: 60,
                        currency: "EUR")

        let ride3 = Ride(company: "Cool Taxi",
                        carNumber: "80",
                        timeInMinutes: 7,
                        rideType: .taxi,
                        price: 25,
                        currency: "EUR")

        return [ ride1, ride2, ride3 ]
    }}
```

In the main `ViewController.swift`, you need to implement the `@IBAction` of the button for finding a route, which will ask the dummy service for the rides. You need a table view as well, which will present the rides, so you will implement the table view data source methods (Listings 2-4 and 2-5). The table view will be fed by the `rides` array of the `Ride` elements.

Listing 2-4. Method called when findRouteButton is tapped

```
// Define at the beginning of the ViewController.
private let rideService = DummyRideService()
private var rides = [Ride]()

@IBAction func findRouteButtonClicked() {
        let fromText = self.checkNil(from?.text as AnyObject?)
        let toText = self.checkNil(to?.text as AnyObject?)
        rideService.findRide(from: fromText, to: toText,
        completion: {
            [unowned self] foundRides in
            self.rides = foundRides
            self.ridesTableView?.reloadData()
        })
 }

func checkNil(_ string: AnyObject?) -> String {
        return string == nil ? "" : string as! String
}
```

Listing 2-5. UITableView's DataSource and Delegate Methods

```
func tableView(_ tableView: UITableView,
                        numberOfRowsInSection section: Int) ->
                        Int {
        return rides.count
}
```

```swift
func tableView(_ tableView: UITableView,
                    cellForRowAt indexPath: IndexPath)
-> UITableViewCell {
        var cell = tableView.dequeueReusableCell(
                withIdentifier: "RouteCell")
        if cell == nil {
            cell = UITableViewCell(style: .default,
                reuseIdentifier: "RouteCell")
        }

        let ride = rides[indexPath.row]
        let displayText =
        "Ride with \(ride.company), car number \(ride.
        carNumber) in \(ride.timeInMinutes) min."
        cell?.textLabel?.text = displayText
        cell?.textLabel?.minimumScaleFactor = 0.3
        cell?.textLabel?.adjustsFontSizeToFitWidth = true

        return cell!
}
```

That's it for the main app. As you can see, it's nothing special. It just presents the found rides. You can run it and test whether it displays the mock rides when the route button is tapped. Now let's start with the interesting part, adding a Siri extension. First, you need to add the Siri capability in the Capabilities section of Xcode for the main app target. This will automatically create an entitlements file with the Siri key set to YES. To run it on a device, you will need to create an app ID that supports Siri and a provisioning profile for that app ID. If everything is set up correctly, you should have all the boxes selected (Figure 2-2).

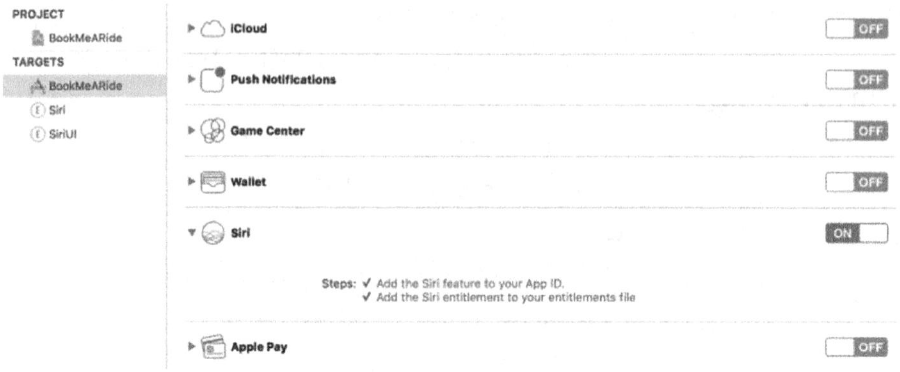

Figure 2-2. *Capabilities section in Xcode with Siri enabled*

The usage of Siri in the app should be transparent to the user—that's why you need to provide a usage description in the Info.plist file. The key is Privacy - Siri Usage Description, and for the value, you will use something like Siri needed for booking a ride. Next, when the screen is shown, you need to check whether the user has authorized Siri (Listing 2-6). This can be done using the INPreferences class, from the Intents framework, which you will explore later in greater detail. Add the method for requesting permission in the viewDidLoad method of the ViewController.

Listing 2-6. Requesting Permission to Use Siri

```
private func requestSiriAuthorization() {
        INPreferences.requestSiriAuthorization {
        authorizationStatus in
            switch authorizationStatus {
            case .authorized:
                print("User authorized Siri")
            default:
                print("User didn't authorize Siri")
            }
        }
}
```

Creating a Siri Extension

The Siri extension is created by adding a new target called the Intents extension (Figure 2-3). The process is similar to adding other types of extensions, such as Apple Watch apps, widgets, and keyboard extensions. In the process of creating the extension, you are asked whether you want to have the Intent UI extension, which is used if you want to modify the default UI displayed in Siri when your app is called. Select that option as well, since you will modify the default user interface. Call the created extension Siri.

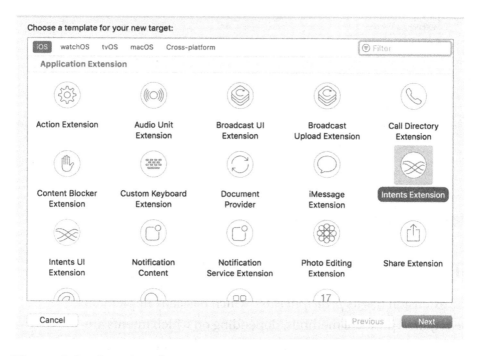

Figure 2-3. *Creating the Intents extension*

After the targets are created, you need to provide in their corresponding `Info.plist` files which extension points you want to support in your app. `INRequestRideIntent` is used to request a ride, and `INGetRideStatusIntent` is used to check the status of a ride; these are what you need in your app. You would use `INListRideOptionsIntent` if you want to provide a ride-booking extension from the Maps app, not Siri. Figure 2-4 shows the `Info.plist` file for your newly created Siri extension.

▼ Information Property List	Dictionary	(10 items)
Localization native development re... ↕	String	en
Bundle display name ↕	String	RoutingSiri
Executable file ↕	String	$(EXECUTABLE_NAME)
Bundle identifier ↕	String	$(PRODUCT_BUNDLE_IDENTIFIER)
InfoDictionary version ↕	String	6.0
Bundle name ↕	String	$(PRODUCT_NAME)
Bundle OS Type code ↕	String	XPC!
Bundle versions string, short ↕	String	1.0
Bundle version ↕	String	1
▼ NSExtension ↕	Dictionary	(3 items)
▼ NSExtensionAttributes	Dictionary	(2 items)
▶ IntentsRestrictedWhileLocked	Array	(0 items)
▼ IntentsSupported ⊕ ⊖	Array ↕	(2 items)
Item 0	String	INRequestRideIntent
Item 1	String	INGetRideStatusIntent
NSExtensionPointIdentifier	String	com.apple.intents-service
NSExtensionPrincipalClass	String	$(PRODUCT_MODULE_NAME).IntentHandler

Figure 2-4. *Info.plist file for the Siri extension*

Implementing the Principal Class

The extension has its *principal class*, which basically implements the required protocol methods, depending on which intents are supported in your app. For example, for the ride-booking feature, you need to conform to the `INRequestRideIntentHandling` and `INGetRideStatusIntentHandling` protocol methods. Figure 2-5 shows the process of implementing the principal class.

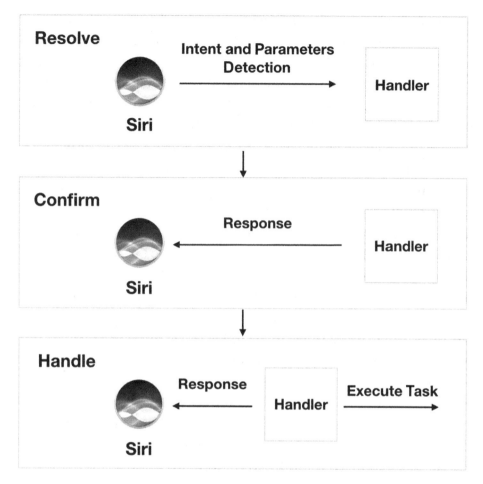

Figure 2-5. *Steps for implementing the principal class*

The first step is *resolve*—where you have to determine whether you can handle the parameters provided by the intent (Siri). The second step is *confirm*, where you are confirming to Siri that you can handle the intent, by providing a response, which contains the details displayed in the Siri pop-up. The responses can be different, depending on what kind of intent you are handling, but they all inherit from the base INIntentResponse. For the ride-booking use case, you need to return INRequestRideIntentResponse, which contains a response code and the ride status. The last step, *handle*, is where you actually perform the action you've confirmed in the previous step. This is the basic overview of the process, although there are additional optional methods you can implement if you want to improve the user experience in the ride-booking process.

The principal class is the `IntentHandler` class, which will conform to the `INRequestRideIntentHandling` and `INGetRideStatusIntentHandling` protocols that need to be implemented for the intents you've registered.

When the user says something like "Hey, Siri, book me a ride," your app will be listed as an option. If the user says "Book me a ride using BookMeARide," then your app will be directly asked to perform this intent. Good practice with conversational user interfaces is to request one piece of information at a time and not proceed to the next step until you get that information. SiriKit follows a similar approach with the `resolvePickupLocation` and `resolveDropOffLocation` actions for the ride intent. If the user, for example, says "Get me a ride to Paris," you should handle the missing pickup location and provide `INPlacemarkResolutionResult` with the `needsValue()` option. This will tell Siri to ask the user for the pickup location. The same applies for the drop-off location ("Get me a ride from London"). If the user provided both values, you are good to go to the next step, and you can resolve both resolution results with success (Listings 2-7 and 2-8). Implement these delegate methods in the `IntentHandler.swift` file.

Listing 2-7. Resolving the Pickup Location in the IntentHandler Class

```
func resolvePickupLocation(
        for intent: INRequestRideIntent,
            with completion:
                @escaping (INPlacemarkResolutionResult) ->
                Void) {
        if (intent.pickupLocation == nil) {
            let result = INPlacemarkResolutionResult.
            needsValue()
```

```
          completion(result)
      } else {
          let result = INPlacemarkResolutionResult.
          success(with: intent.pickupLocation!)
          completion(result)
      }
}
```

Listing 2-8. Resolving the Drop-Off Location

```
func resolveDropOffLocation(
      for intent: INRequestRideIntent,
          with completion:
              @escaping (INPlacemarkResolutionResult) ->
              Void) {
      if (intent.dropOffLocation == nil) {
          let result = INPlacemarkResolutionResult.
          needsValue()
          completion(result)
      } else {
          let result = INPlacemarkResolutionResult.
          success(with: intent.dropOffLocation!)
          completion(result)
      }
}
```

Next, when you have the starting and ending locations, you need to ask for the type of ride the user wants—taxi or limo. For this, you will implement the `resolveRideOptionName` method (Listing 2-9), also in the `IntentHandler` class. If the user hasn't specified the type of ride wanted, you will resolve the result with a disambiguation, and Siri will present the user with the two options you support. If the user was precise enough, saying something like "Get me a taxi from Cambridge to London," you can resolve the intent with success and proceed to confirming the ride.

Listing 2-9. Resolving the Ride Option

```
func resolveRideOptionName(
        for intent: INRequestRideIntent,
          with completion:
            @escaping (INSpeakableStringResolutionResult) ->
            Void) {
        if let rideOption = intent.rideOptionName {
            let result = INSpeakableStringResolutionResult.
            success(with: rideOption)
            completion(result)
        } else {
            let first = INSpeakableString(
                            identifier: IntentHandler.
                            taxiIdentifier,
                                    spokenPhrase: "Taxi",
                                    pronunciationHint: nil)
            let second = INSpeakableString(
                            identifier: IntentHandler.
                            limoIdentifier,
                                    spokenPhrase: "Limo",
                                    pronunciationHint: nil)
            let result = INSpeakableStringResolutionResult.
            disambiguation(with: [first, second])
            completion(result)
        }
}
```

Figure 2-6 shows the user interface that Siri presents when asking the user to provide the ride option.

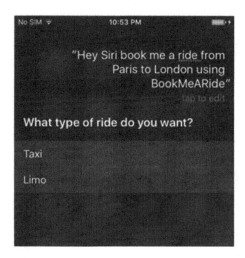

Figure 2-6. *Selecting the type of ride*

After you have gathered all the information you need to reserve a ride for your user, you need to implement the confirmation of the ride. This is to check whether you can execute the user's intent (Listing 2-10).

Listing 2-10. Confirming Whether You Can Handle the Intent

```
func confirm(intent: INRequestRideIntent,
                    completion:
                    @escaping (INRequestRideIntentResponse) ->
                    Void) {
        self.handleIntent(requestRide: intent, completion:
        completion)
}
```

If the extension confirms that it can handle the intent, Siri will show a confirmation screen, where the user has the chance to book the ride (Figure 2-7).

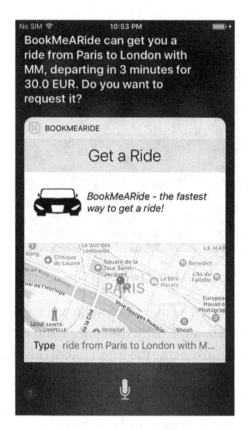

Figure 2-7. *Siri providing a ride option to the user*

Before you proceed with the handleIntent implementation, let's first define some variables and constants that you will use in the method (Listing 2-11).

Listing 2-11. Defining Variables and Constants in the IntentHandler Class

```
let rideService = DummyRideService()
static let taxiIdentifier = "Taxi"
static let limoIdentifier = "Limo"
static let rideOptionKey = "rideOption"
```

```
static let pickupDateKey = "pickupDate"
static let statusKey = "status"
```

You are now ready to explore the handleIntent method, where the logic for the confirmation of the ride is implemented (Listing 2-12).

Listing 2-12. Handling the Ride Booking Intent

```
private func handleIntent(requestRide intent:
INRequestRideIntent,
completion:
                @escaping (INRequestRideIntentResponse) -> Void) {
        let userActivity =
            NSUserActivity(activityType: NSStringFromClass(INRe
            questRideIntentResponse.self))
        var response = INRequestRideIntentResponse(code:
                        .success,

                        userActivity: userActivity)
        let from = intent.pickupLocation?.name
        let to = intent.dropOffLocation?.name
        var rideType: RideType = .taxi
        if let phrase = intent.rideOptionName?.spokenPhrase {
            if phrase == IntentHandler.limoIdentifier {
                rideType = .limo
            }
        }
        if let from = from, let to = to {
            rideService.findRide(from: from, to: to, completion: {
            [unowned self] rides in
                if rides.count > 0 {
                    let rideStatus = self.
                    convertRidesToRideStatus(rides: rides,
    from: from,
```

```
    to: to,
  rideType: rideType)
                let rideInfo: [String : Any] =
                    [ IntentHandler.rideOptionKey :
                    rideStatus.rideOption!.name,
                      IntentHandler.pickupDateKey
                      : rideStatus.rideOption!.
                      estimatedPickupDate]
                RideStorage.removeRide()
                RideStorage.save(rideInfo: rideInfo)
                response.rideStatus = rideStatus
                completion(response)
            } else {
                response = INRequestRideIntentResponse(code:
                        .failure,

                        userActivity: userActivity)
                            RideStorage.removeRide()
                            completion(response)

            }
        })
    } else {
        response = INRequestRideIntentResponse(code:
                .failure,

                userActivity: userActivity)
        RideStorage.removeRide()
        completion(response)
    }
}
```

There is a lot going on in the handleIntent method, so let's analyze it step-by-step. First, you are creating the response object (INRequestRideIntentResponse) with a user activity and status code.

The user activity is needed in cases when the user opens the app from Siri (this usually happens when an error occurs). In the user activity, you can pass some context and prepare your app to proceed at the place where the error with Siri happened. You can access the user activity from the didFinishLaunchingWithOptions method with Listing 2-13.

Listing 2-13. Handling the User Activity Passed from Siri

```
if let activityDic =
    launchOptions?[UIApplicationLaunchOptionsUserActivity
    DictionaryKey]
            as? [NSObject : AnyObject],
    activity = activityDic["UIApplicationLaunchOptionsUser
            ActivityKey"]
            as? NSUserActivity {
    handleActivity(activity)
}
```

The status code supports many options, such as success, ready, in progress, and a few failure codes (Listing 2-14).

Listing 2-14. Supported status codes for the ride intent response

```
public enum INRequestRideIntentResponseCode : Int {
    case unspecified
    case ready
    @available(iOS, introduced: 10.0, deprecated: 11.0,
    message: "INRequestRideIntentResponseCodeInProgress is
    deprecated.")
    case inProgress
    case success
    case failure
    case failureRequiringAppLaunch
    case failureRequiringAppLaunchMustVerifyCredentials
```

```
    case failureRequiringAppLaunchNoServiceInArea
    case failureRequiringAppLaunchServiceTemporarilyUnavailable
    case failureRequiringAppLaunchPreviousRideNeedsCompletion
}
```

You assume that it is successful at the beginning, and if there's an error, you will update it accordingly. Next, you read the `pickup` and `dropOff` locations for the ride and the ride option name and based on that decide on the ride type. Then, you ask your ride service (in this case, `DummyRideService`) to give you a list of possible rides for this route. If there are rides available, you create a ride status based on the provided information (I will get back to this method shortly). Next, you save the ride to `RideStorage` (defined later in the chapter in Listing 2-17). You need this for getting the status of the ride. At the end, you return the completion handler with a successful response. In any other case, you complete the handler with a failure code.

Now, let's see how you can create the ride status. The `convertRidesToRideStatus` method does that (Listing 2-15).

Listing 2-15. Converting Rides to Ride Statuses

```
private func convertRidesToRideStatus(rides: [Ride],
                                      from: String,
                                      to: String,
                                      rideType: RideType)
                                      -> INRideStatus {
        var text = "ride "
        var selectedRide = rides.first!
        for ride in rides {
            if ride.rideType == rideType {
                selectedRide = ride
                break
            }
        }
```

```
let price = "\(selectedRide.price) \(selectedRide.
currency)"
let minutes = Int(selectedRide.timeInMinutes)
text += "from \(from) to \(to) with \(selectedRide.
company), " +
        "departing in \(minutes) minutes for \(price)"
let rideStatus = INRideStatus()
let pickupDate = Date().addingTimeInterval(selectedRide.
timeInMinutes * 60)
rideStatus.rideOption = INRideOption(name: text,
estimatedPickupDate: pickupDate)

return rideStatus
}
```

You first check whether there's a ride with the provided ride type. If there's no such ride, you provide the first option to the user (which is a different ride type, but the user might still be interested). Then, you read the price, the currency, and the estimated time. This information is needed for the text of the ride option that will be read to the user by Siri. This is represented by the INRideOption object, which is part of the ride status.

If the user wants to book the ride that Siri provided via your app, the handle(intent:,completion) method is called, which actually performs the ride reservation (Listing 2-16). This is the place where you will call a REST service with a request to reserve the ride, but since you are working with dummy rides here, you will just save to the RideStorage class that the ride is confirmed. You will also create a ride status with the confirmed ride phase. This will tell Siri to present a confirmation screen.

Listing 2-16. Handling the Request Ride Intent

```
func handle(intent: INRequestRideIntent,
            completion:
            @escaping (INRequestRideIntentResponse) -> Void) {
```

```
    let userActivity = NSUserActivity(activityType: NSStrin
    gFromClass(INRequestRideIntentResponse.self))
    let response = INRequestRideIntentResponse(code:
    .success,
                        userActivity: userActivity)
    let rideStatus = INRideStatus()
    rideStatus.phase = INRidePhase.confirmed
    RideStorage.save(rideInfo: [ IntentHandler.statusKey :
    true ])
    rideStatus.pickupLocation = intent.pickupLocation
    rideStatus.dropOffLocation = intent.dropOffLocation
    let pickupDate = RideStorage.latestRide()?[IntentHandler.
    pickupDateKey] as! Date
    rideStatus.rideOption =
        INRideOption(name: (intent.rideOptionName?.
        spokenPhrase)!,
                        estimatedPickupDate: pickupDate)

    response.rideStatus = rideStatus
    completion(response)
}
```

I have mentioned the RideStorage class. This is just a wrapper around
UserDefaults; it has methods to save and remove a ride (you are supporting
only one ride at a time) and also returns the latest ride (Listing 2-17).

Listing 2-17. RideStorage Class

```
class RideStorage {
    static let savedRideId = "savedRide"

    class func save(rideInfo: [String : Any]) {
        var newRideInfo = rideInfo
        if let saved = latestRide() {
```

```
            newRideInfo.merge(with: saved)
        }
        UserDefaults.standard.set(newRideInfo,
                                                forKey:
RideStorage.savedRideId)
        UserDefaults.standard.synchronize()
    }

    class func removeRide() {
        UserDefaults.standard.set(nil, forKey: RideStorage.
        savedRideId)
        UserDefaults.standard.synchronize()
    }

    class func latestRide() -> [String : Any]? {
        return UserDefaults.standard.value(forKey: RideStorage.
        savedRideId) as? [String : Any]
    }
}
```

In the save method, if there is already a ride, you merge its contents with the new one. For this, you need to define additional methods in Apple's Dictionary class (Listing 2-18).

Listing 2-18. Providing Merge Methods to the Dictionary Class

```
extension Dictionary {

    mutating func merge(with dictionary: Dictionary) {
        dictionary.forEach { updateValue($1, forKey: $0) }
    }

    func merged(with dictionary: Dictionary) -> Dictionary {
        var dict = self
        dict.merge(with: dictionary)
```

```
        return dict
    }
}
```

If you run the Siri extension now (by selecting the appropriate Siri target from Xcode's run menu), provide a sample phrase, and confirm the ride, you should get a confirmation screen like the one in Figure 2-8.

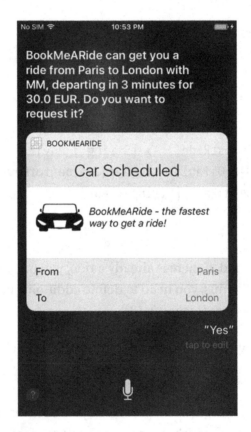

Figure 2-8. *Confirmed ride*

Checking the Status of a Ride

After the user has confirmed the ride, they might be interested in checking the status of the ride (Figure 2-9). One phrase that supports this is "How far is my ride using BookMeARide?"

Figure 2-9. *Checking the status of a ride*

Let's see how you can implement this. When the user provides a voice command that is recognized as part of the INGetRideStatusIntent domain, the method in Listing 2-19 is called.

Listing 2-19. Handling the Status of a Ride

```
public func handle(intent: INGetRideStatusIntent,
                   completion:
              @escaping (INGetRideStatusIntentResponse) -> Void) {
    guard let latest = RideStorage.latestRide() else {
        failureResponse(completion: completion)
        return
    }

    guard let status = latest[IntentHandler.statusKey] as?
    Bool else {
        failureResponse(completion: completion)
        return
    }

    guard status == true else {
        failureResponse(completion: completion)
        return
    }

    let response = INGetRideStatusIntentResponse(code: .success,
                   userActivity: nil)
    let rideStatus = INRideStatus()
    let pickupDate = latest[IntentHandler.pickupDateKey]
    as! Date
    rideStatus.rideOption =
        INRideOption(
            name: latest[IntentHandler.rideOptionKey] as!
            String,
                    estimatedPickupDate: pickupDate)
    rideStatus.phase = ridePhase(forPickupDate: pickupDate)
```

```
        response.rideStatus = rideStatus
        completion(response)
    }

    private func failureResponse(completion:
                @escaping (INGetRideStatusIntentResponse) -> Void) {
        let response = INGetRideStatusIntentResponse(code:
        .failure, userActivity: nil)
        completion(response)
    }
```

What happens here? You check whether there's a ride available in your RideStorage class and whether there's a positive status code for that ride. If there's not, you will provide a response to the user that you currently don't have any rides available. Otherwise, you will take the estimated pickup date and compare it with the current date. Based on the difference, the status of the ride will have different value. The ridePhaseMethod does that (Listing 2-20).

Listing 2-20. Determining the Phase of the Ride

```
private func ridePhase(forPickupDate date: Date) -> INRidePhase
{
    let dateDiff = self.dateDiff(forPickupDate: date)
    if dateDiff < 0 {
        return .ongoing
    } else {
        if dateDiff > 60 {
            return .approachingPickup
        } else {
            return .pickup
        }
    }
}
```

```
private func dateDiff(forPickupDate date: Date) -> Int {
    let dateDiff = Calendar.current.dateComponents([.second],
                      from: Date(),
                      to: date).second ?? 0
    return dateDiff
}
```

If the date difference is less than zero, then the car should've already arrived, which is why you return the ongoing ride phase. If the car is 60 or more seconds away, you return the approachingPickup phase, and if it's less than that, you return the pickup phase, which means the car is close and ready.

You can also send updates to Siri about the status of the ride. For this, you will need to have a real-time ride service, which will provide you with information, in certain periods of time, about how far the ride is from the user. Listing 2-21 lists the methods that allow you to notify Siri about the status of the ride.

Listing 2-21. Start and Stop Sending Updates to Siri About the Status of the Ride

```
public func startSendingUpdates(
              for intent: INGetRideStatusIntent,
                  to observer:
INGetRideStatusIntentResponseObserver) {
      print("Siri started asking for updates for the ride")
}

public func stopSendingUpdates(for intent:
INGetRideStatusIntent) {
      print("Siri stopped asking for updates for the ride")
}
```

That's all you need to do to check the status of the ride. Run the extension and provide a sample phrase to check the status of the ride. If you've noticed in the screenshots, there's also a little branding part in the Siri screens of the BookMeARide app—a logo and a catchy slogan promising the fastest way to get a ride (Figure 2-10).

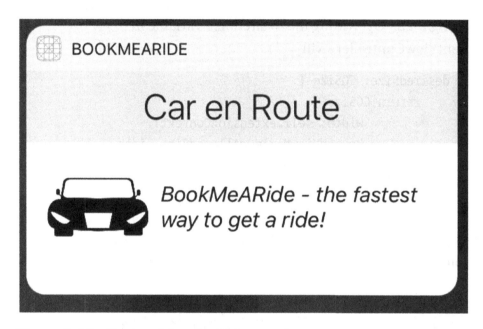

Figure 2-10. *Customizing the Siri extension*

This is done by creating the `SiriUI` target. In this target, you have an `IntentViewController`, which provides a way to configure the size of the views that will be presented in the space reserved for a custom UI in the Siri pop-up. There's also a storyboard file, where you can put images and text, just like in iOS apps. I've put a logo and a tagline for this awesome app. One restriction here is that you cannot pass the data from the `IntentHandler` class to this view, so the data presented here is mostly static. You cannot, for example, create a list of all available rides and put them in a table view in the supplementary section of the pop-up.

In the `IntentViewController` in the UI extension, you need to override the `desiredSize` variable for Siri to know how much space you need for the custom part (Listing 2-22). For the custom UI, you will need a height of 100 points and the maximum width that Siri allows, depending on the screen's width.

Listing 2-22. Overriding the desiredSize Variable in IntentViewController.swift

```
var desiredSize: CGSize {
        return CGSize(
                width: self.extensionContext!.
                hostedViewMaximumAllowedSize.width,
                height: 100)
}
```

That's everything you need to do to book a ride using Siri. Now, let's see how you can teach Siri to learn customized phrases for your application.

Building a Custom App Vocabulary

Sometimes you will want to provide custom words or phrases that are specific to your application or let the user define their own phrases to perform some actions or identify contacts. For example, users might want to call someone referencing them by their nickname. Parents can say "Send money to my son or daughter." Also, there are cases where your app has fancy name that might not even be a proper English word. These custom words can be provided with the INVocabulary API to Siri, which will learn those words and associate them with your app. The words or intents that are valid for all users of your app can be declared in the global vocabulary of the application. The ones that are user specific must be provided from the main application (not from the Siri extension) using methods from the INVocabulary API. If you support multiple languages, you can include localized versions of your vocabulary property list file in the language-specific project (.lproj) directories of your app.

Note   The user-specific custom words that Siri needs to learn are provided from the main application through the INVocabulary API.

Creating a Global App Vocabulary

To have a global vocabulary file, you should create a new property list file and call it AppIntentVocabulary.plist. Add the file to the main iOS application. The created property list file has two keys at the root level.

- IntentPhrases, which contains an array of example intent phrases for invoking features of the application

- ParameterVocabularies, which has an array of phrases common to all users of the application

The IntentPhrases array consists of dictionaries, which contain the following keys:

- IntentName: This is the name of the intent for which this example phrase applies. The value here has to match the exact name of an intent. You should take this value from the IntentsSupported array defined in the Info.plist file of your Siri extension. For example, if you want to define a different phrase for requesting a ride from the BookMeARide app, you should add INRequestRideIntent as a value here.

- `IntentExamples`: This is an array of sample phrases that will complement the default ones. Here is the place where you define the custom phrases. As example phrases, you can add sentences like "Can you find me a ride," "Reserve me a ride," "I want a ride," and similar. The next time the user says such a phrase, the BookMeARide app will be invoked. If your app is the only one that supports that phrase, the user doesn't even have to specify the name of the app; they can just say the phrase (Figure 2-11).

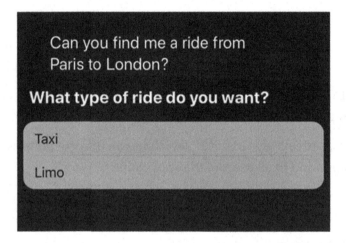

Figure 2-11. *Reserving a ride with a custom phrase*

Figure 2-12 shows the `AppIntentVocabulary` property list file.

▼ App Intent Vocabulary Property List		Dictionary	(2 items)
▼ Intent Phrases	⬍	Array	(1 item)
▼ Item 0 (Intent Phrase)		Dictionary	(2 items)
Intent Name	⬍	String	INRequestRideIntent
▼ Intent Examples	⬍	Array	(3 items)
Item 0 (Intent Example)		String	Can you find me a ride
Item 1 (Intent Example)		String	Reserve me a ride
Item 2 (Intent Example)		String	I want a ride

Figure 2-12. *Defining custom phrases for booking a ride*

Now, let's look at the `ParameterVocabularies` array. As mentioned, with this array you can specify some terms that are valid for all users of the application. This array also contains dictionaries, with the following keys:

- `ParameterNames`: This is an array of key paths for property names from an intent class. This might sound abstract; I'll explain it with an example. Let's say that instead of New York, you want to say "Book me a ride to the Big Apple." You want to provide another phrase (synonym) for the city of New York for the location property. There are two types of location in the ride-booking intent (pickup location and drop-off location), so you provide these two values as parameter names. Since they are `CLPlacemark` objects, you should add their name property in the parameter name.

- `ParameterVocabulary`: This is an array of dictionaries that contain the mapping between the original word and the synonym. `VocabularyItemIdentifier` contains information about the original word or phrase recognized by Siri. In this case, that would be `New York`. Next, you need to provide the synonyms, using the `VocabularyItemSynonyms` array of dictionaries. In these dictionaries, it is required that you provide `VocabularyItemPhrase`, which is the custom phrase that the app will use. In the New York example, that would be the `Big Apple`. You can also define pronunciation hints for the phrase, using the `VocabularyItemPronunciation` key. The hints should sound like the string, not be how it is written. For example, if you are developing a music app and you want to define a custom phrase for the band U2, the pronunciation hint would be "you too."

There is also the ability to provide an array of strings that contain examples of how to use the phrase (VocabularyItemExamples).

With these changes, you can say something like "Can you find me a ride from Paris to the Big Apple?" and Siri would be able to determine that you need a ride from Paris to New York (Figure 2-13).

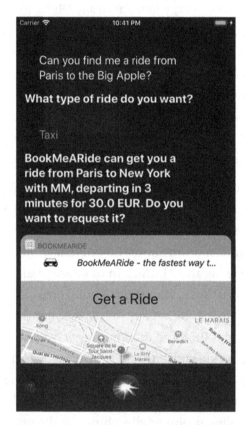

Figure 2-13. *Booking a ride with a custom phrase*

Figure 2-14 shows an excerpt of the AppIntentVocabulary.plist file with the synonym entries.

▼ Parameter Vocabularies	↕	Array	(1 item)
▼ Item 0 (Parameter Vocabulary)		Dictionary	(2 items)
▼ Parameter Names	↕	Array	(2 items)
Item 0 (Parameter Name)		String	INRequestRideIntent.dropOffLocation.name
Item 1 (Parameter Name)		String	INRequestRideIntent.pickupLocation.name
▼ Parameter Vocabulary	↕	Array	(1 item)
▼ Item 0 (Parameter Vocabulary)		Dictionary	(2 items)
Vocabulary Item Identifier	↕	String	**New York**
▼ Vocabulary Item Synonyms	↕	Array	(1 item)
▼ Item 0 (Vocabulary Item Synonym)		Dictionary	(1 item)
Vocabulary Item Phrase	↕	String	**Big Apple**

Figure 2-14. *Parameter vocabularies*

Providing App Name Synonyms

You can also provide other names for your app. This might simplify users' interaction with your app. These alternative names should not include names of other apps installed on the phone to prevent taking over requests for those apps. To define synonyms for your app name, you should include the INAlternativeAppNames key in the Info.plist file of the main iOS application. This key has an array of dictionaries with these two keys:

- INAlternativeAppName: This is the synonym name that the users can use to invoke your app.

- INAlternativeAppNamePronunciationHint: This is an optional hint on how to pronounce the app name.

For example, if you want users to access your app with the "using CoolRide" phrase, your Info.plist file should look like Figure 2-15.

▼ Information Property List		Dictionary	(16 items)
▼ INAlternativeAppNames	↕	Array	(1 item)
▼ Item 0		Dictionary	(2 items)
INAlternativeAppName		String	CoolRide
INAlternativeAppNamePronunci...		String	cool ride

Figure 2-15. *Alternative app names*

Allowing a User-Specific Vocabulary

In addition to the globally defined words and phrases, you can also let users define phrases that are relevant only to them. You can do this by using the INVocabulary API, which should be called from the main application. The INVocabulary API is pretty simple and contains three methods. The first two are available from iOS 10, while the third one can be used only on iOS 11.

The setVocabularyString:ofType method accepts an ordered set of Strings for a given INVocabularyStringType. The vocabulary string types are restricted to certain categories, such as contact names, photo albums, workout names, payment organization names, and so on. For example, you can't provide a user-specific name for the pickup or drop-off location in the ride-booking domain like you did with the global app vocabulary. The vocabulary strings are an ordered set, which means the ones at the beginning of the set have a higher priority. How does this work? Let's say you have an app that sends messages. If you have one of your parents saved as a contact with their first and last names but you want to send messages by saying "mom" or "dad," these values should be provided in the ordered set, and Siri would be able to provide them in INSendMessageIntent.

You can remove all the vocabulary strings by calling the method removeAllVocabularyStrings.

The problem with these iOS 10 methods is that you have only strings in the set, without additional context to them. For example, you have to do some custom mapping to find out that the phrase "mom" or "dad" corresponds to a certain contact in the list.

For this reason, starting from iOS 11, there is a new method, called setVocabulary:ofType:, where you provide objects that implement the INSpeakeable protocol, instead of plain strings. The INSpeakable protocol provides more details about the entries that Siri tries to learn. Objects that implement the protocol should provide the spoken phrase, a pronunciation hint, and a vocabulary identifier (which can be a unique identifier for the object). You can also provide alternative INSpeakeable vocabulary items using the `alternativeSpeakeableMatches` array.

With this approach, the matching of the detected alternative words is much simpler on the app side. Let's see an example. You will create a new class, `VocabularyItem`, that implements the `INSpeakable` protocol (Listing 2-23).

Listing 2-23. Implementing INSpeakable Protocol

```
class VocabularyItem: NSObject, INSpeakable {
    var spokenPhrase: String

    var pronunciationHint: String?

    var vocabularyIdentifier: String?

    var alternativeSpeakableMatches: [INSpeakable]?

    init(spokenPhrase: String,
         vocabularyIdentifier: String?,
         pronunciationHint: String?) {
        self.spokenPhrase = spokenPhrase
        self.vocabularyIdentifier = vocabularyIdentifier
        self.pronunciationHint = pronunciationHint
    }
}
```

Then, when the user selects (through an appropriate user interface) which words should also have alternative phrases, you can call a method like the one in Listing 2-24.

Listing 2-24. Saving a Vocabulary Item

```
func saveVocabularyItem(spokenPhrase: String, originalWord:
String) {
    let vocabularyItem = VocabularyItem(spokenPhrase: spokenPhrase,
                                    vocabularyIdentifier:
                                    originalWord,
                                    pronunciationHint:
                                    spokenPhrase)
    var savedVocabularyItems = self.loadVocabularyItems()
    savedVocabularyItems.insert(vocabularyItem, at: 0)
    INVocabulary.shared().setVocabulary(savedVocabularyItems,
                                    of: .contactName)
}

func loadVocabularyItems() -> NSOrderedSet {
        // load items, perhaps from UserDefaults
        return []
}
```

As you can see, the INVocabulary API is pretty straightforward and gives you quick wins for designing a better user experience.

Summary

SiriKit enables third-party apps to provide functionality that can be executed in Siri, without starting the app. The speech-recognizing part and the natural language understanding is already done by SiriKit, which means you can take the already recognized values and focus on implementing the business rules of your application. However, SiriKit also comes with limitations; you can use it only in predefined domains. If your app doesn't provide functionality related to those domains, then you can't use SiriKit.

In the chapter, you created a simple iOS app that returns predefined rides. Then you created the Siri extension, which supports the ride-booking domain. By implementing the provided delegate methods of the ride-booking intent handling, you were able to extract everything you needed to know about the user's request for a ride—pickup location, drop-off location, and ride option.

You also implemented the delegate methods for checking the status of the ride, giving the user the ability to check on the ride. By using the SiriUI extension, you were also able to customize the user interface presented in Siri. Then, you saw how you can teach Siri to learn new words and phrases that are specific to your app or to certain users of the app. In the next chapter, you will develop another SiriKit project from a different domain.

CHAPTER 3

Creating Lists with SiriKit

Another interesting domain is lists and notes, which encompasses adding and removing items to and from a to-do list as well as adding notes. It's a really handy domain, which you will explore in detail in this chapter. You will create an app that can add and remove items to and from a grocery list. Later in the chapter, you will see how you can write UI tests to verify whether your Siri implementation is correct.

Overview of the App

Let's create a new single-view application in Xcode and call it ListsSiriKit. The user interface of the main iOS application is really simple, with two screens (Figure 3-1). The first screen shows the lists that the user has created in a table view. When a list is selected, it opens a new screen with the tasks that it contains. Both screens contain a button for adding items to the table view (lists in the first screen or tasks in the second screen). There is a starter project for this chapter, where the user interface and the initial setup are already prepared for you, so you can easily get started developing the cool features of your application.

© Martin Mitrevski 2018
M. Mitrevski, *Developing Conversational Interfaces for iOS*,
https://doi.org/10.1007/978-1-4842-3396-2_3

Figure 3-1. *User interface for the to-do list app*

The data in the main app will be synchronized with the Siri extension—whenever the user does an update (adds or removes a list or task) from Siri, the change should be reflected in the main app. Let's first create the Intents extension (you already know how to do this from the previous chapter).

Next, update the `Info.plist` file of the Siri extension so it knows which intents you are going to support in your app. Your app will support creating lists, adding tasks to a list, and marking tasks as completed. To have these functionalities, you will need to add the `INCreateTaskListIntent`, `INAddTasksIntent`, and `INSetTaskAttributeIntent` intents to your `Info. plist` file (Figure 3-2).

Key	Type	Value
⊞ ⟨ ⟩ 🖼 ListsSiriKit ⟩ ▦ Siri ⟩ 🗒 Info.plist ⟩ No Selection		
Key	Type	Value
▼ Information Property List	Dictionary	(10 items)
Localization native development r... ⬦	String	$(DEVELOPMENT_LANGUAGE)
Bundle display name ⬦	String	Siri
Executable file ⬦	String	$(EXECUTABLE_NAME)
Bundle identifier ⬦	String	$(PRODUCT_BUNDLE_IDENTIFIER)
InfoDictionary version ⬦	String	6.0
Bundle name ⬦	String	$(PRODUCT_NAME)
Bundle OS Type code ⬦	String	XPC!
Bundle versions string, short ⬦	String	1.0
Bundle version ⬦	String	1
▼ NSExtension ⬦	Dictionary	(3 items)
▼ NSExtensionAttributes	Dictionary	(2 items)
▶ IntentsRestrictedWhileLocked	Array	(0 items)
▼ IntentsSupported	Array	(3 items)
Item 0	String	INCreateTaskListIntent
Item 1	String	INAddTasksIntent
Item 2	String	INSetTaskAttributeIntent
NSExtensionPointIdentifier	String	com.apple.intents-service
NSExtensionPrincipalClass	String	$(PRODUCT_MODULE_NAME).IntentHandler

Figure 3-2. *Supported intents for the lists domain*

Caution   Although an app extension bundle is nested in the containing app's bundle, the app extension and the main app have no direct access to each other's containers.

App Groups

The next challenge to tackle is where to store the data the user creates so it's accessible from both the main app and the Siri extension. Since you are storing the data only locally (you don't have a back end), shared user defaults are a good option. To support this, you need to create an app group, which then needs to be added to both targets. But to configure an app group, you will first need to create an app ID from Apple's developer portal (Figure 3-3).

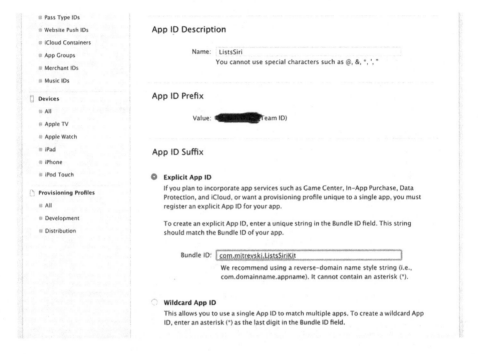

Figure 3-3. *Creating an app ID*

Why do you need this app group? The main app and its extension don't have access to the corresponding app containers, so there has to be a mechanism to share or pass data between them. The solution is a shared container, which can be accessed by both apps using app groups.

Now that you know the importance of app groups, let's enable them for the created app ID (Figure 3-4).

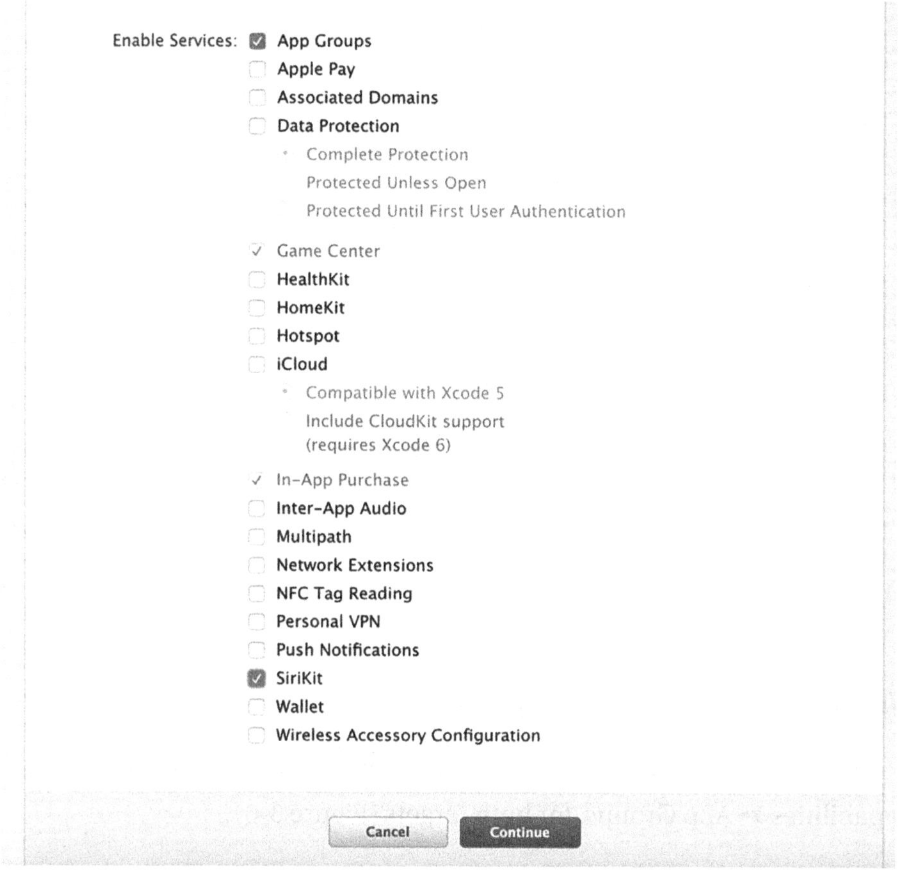

Enable Services: ☑ App Groups
                  ☐ Apple Pay
                  ☐ Associated Domains
                  ☐ Data Protection
                     ⦁ Complete Protection
                       Protected Unless Open
                       Protected Until First User Authentication
                  ☑ Game Center
                  ☐ HealthKit
                  ☐ HomeKit
                  ☐ Hotspot
                  ☐ iCloud
                     ⦁ Compatible with Xcode 5
                       Include CloudKit support
                       (requires Xcode 6)
                  ☑ In–App Purchase
                  ☐ Inter–App Audio
                  ☐ Multipath
                  ☐ Network Extensions
                  ☐ NFC Tag Reading
                  ☐ Personal VPN
                  ☐ Push Notifications
                  ☑ SiriKit
                  ☐ Wallet
                  ☐ Wireless Accessory Configuration

Cancel   Continue

Figure 3-4. *Enabling app groups for an application ID*

Then, under Identifiers, go to App Groups and create a new group ID with a unique identifier and add this new group ID to the app ID you just created (Figure 3-5).

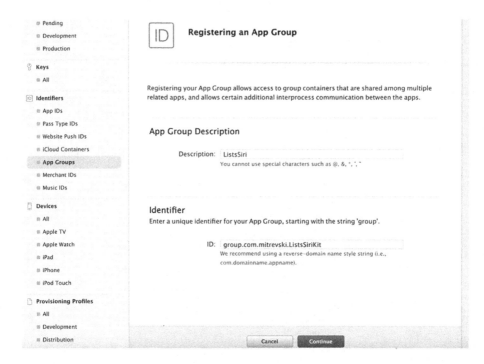

Figure 3-5. *Registering an app group*

If everything is set up correctly, you should see all check marks under Capabilities ➤ App Groups, for both targets (Figure 3-6).

▼ ⊕⊕ **App Groups**   ⎡ ON ⎤

App Groups: ☑ group.com.mitrevski.ListsSiriKit

                    ＋ ↻

Steps: ✓ Add the App Groups entitlement to your entitlements file
            ✓ Add the App Groups feature to your App ID.

            ✓ Add App Groups to your App ID

Figure 3-6. *App groups in the Capabilities section*

Now, you can load the user defaults with the group ID as a suite name, and all the data between the app and the extension will be synced. You will create a new class, called `ListsManager`, which will handle all the changes in the user's data—the creation and modification of the lists and tasks (Listing 3-1).

Listing 3-1. ListsManager Implementation

```
class ListsManager {
    private var savedLists: [String : [String]] = [String :
    [String]]()
    static let ListsKey = "lists"
    static let GroupId = "group.com.mitrevski.ListsSiriKit"
    static let sharedInstance = ListsManager()
    let sharedDefaults = UserDefaults(suiteName: ListsManager.
    GroupId)

    init() {
        if let saved =
                sharedDefaults?.value(forKey: ListsManager.
                ListsKey) {
            savedLists = saved as! [String : [String]]
        }
    }

    func lists() -> [String : [String]] {
        return savedLists
    }

    func tasksForList(withName name: String) -> [String] {
        if let tasks = savedLists[name] {
            return tasks
        }
        return []
    }
```

```swift
func createList(name: String) {
    let list = [String]()
    updateSavedLists(changedList: list, listName: name)
}

func deleteList(name: String) {
    updateSavedLists(changedList: nil, listName: name)
}

func add(tasks: [String], toList listName: String) {
    var list = savedLists[listName] == nil ? [] :
    savedLists[listName]!
    list.append(contentsOf: tasks)
    updateSavedLists(changedList: list, listName: listName)
}

func finish(task: String) {
    if let listName = self.findTaskInList(withName: task) {
        var list = savedLists[listName]!
        if let index = list.index(of: task) {
            list.remove(at: index)
            updateSavedLists(changedList: list, listName:
            listName)
        }
    }
}

private func updateSavedLists(changedList: [String]?,
listName: String) {
    savedLists[listName] = changedList
    sharedDefaults?.set(savedLists, forKey: ListsManager.
    ListsKey)
    sharedDefaults?.synchronize()
}
```

```
    private func findTaskInList(withName taskName: String) ->
    String? {
        for (listName, list) in savedLists {
            if list.contains(taskName) {
                return listName
            }
        }
        return nil
    }
}
```

In the ViewController, you need to implement the table view data source and delegate methods by using the methods defined in the ListsManager (Listing 3-2). You enable the ability to delete a list by swiping from right to left, by implementing the tableView(_,commit editingStyle, forRowAt:) method. When a list is selected, you show the tasks associated with that list, by performing the showTasks segue.

Listing 3-2. Table View Data Source and Delegate Methods in ViewController.swift

```
func tableView(_ tableView: UITableView,
               canEditRowAt indexPath: IndexPath)
-> Bool {
    return true
}

func tableView(_ tableView: UITableView,
               commit editingStyle:
               UITableViewCellEditingStyle,
               forRowAt indexPath: IndexPath) {
    if editingStyle == .delete {
        let listName = Array(ListsManager.sharedInstance.
        lists().keys)[indexPath.row]
```

```
                ListsManager.sharedInstance.deleteList(name:
                listName)
                self.tableView.reloadData()
        }
}

func tableView(_ tableView: UITableView,
               didSelectRowAt indexPath: IndexPath) {
    tableView.deselectRow(at: indexPath, animated: true)
    selectedRow = indexPath
    self.performSegue(withIdentifier: "showTasks", sender: self)
}
```

You also have to provide the implementation when the button for adding lists is tapped, which will display a pop-up where the user can enter the name of the list and save it. When the next screen appears, which is represented by the TasksViewController, you need to pass the information about which list is selected from the ViewController. To accomplish this, you implement the prepare(for segue:, sender:) method (Listing 3-3).

Listing 3-3. Implementing the Action When the addButton Is Tapped and Passing List Name Data to the Next Screen

```
@IBAction func addButtonClicked(sender: UIBarButtonItem) {
        let alertController = self.alertForAddingItems()
        self.present(alertController, animated: true,
        completion: nil)
}

private func alertForAddingItems() -> UIAlertController {
        let alertController = ListsSiriKit.alertForAddingItems(
                                title: "Please provide list name",
```

```
                                        placeholder:
                                        "List name")
        return addActions(toAlertController: alertController,
                        saveActionHandler: { [unowned self]
                        action in
                            let textField = alertController.
                            textFields![0]
                            if let text = textField.text {
                                if text != "" {
                                    ListsManager.
                                    sharedInstance.createList(
                                    name: text)
                                    self.tableView.reloadData()
                                }
                            }
                            alertController.dismiss(animated:
                            true, completion: nil)
        })
}

override func prepare(for segue: UIStoryboardSegue, sender:
Any?) {
        if segue.identifier == "showTasks" {
            let next = segue.destination as!
            TasksViewController
            let listName = Array(ListsManager.sharedInstance.
            lists().keys)[selectedRow!.row]
            next.listName = listName
            selectedRow = nil
        }
}
```

The `alertForAddingItems` method retrieves the text from the `textField` in the `alertController` and creates a list, using the `ListManager`. Since similar functionality with a pop-up and a text field will be needed in the other screen as well, you are using the utility method `alertForAddingItems(title:, placeholder:)`, which creates the `alertController` with a title and placeholder (for the text field). Since the two pop-ups will have similar Save and Cancel actions, you are abstracting that logic as well. In the `addActions(toAlertController:, saveActionHandler:)`, the save action is passed as a parameter because that would be the only difference between the two pop-ups. Add these two methods in a new file, called `Utils.swift` (Listing 3-4).

Listing 3-4. Utility Methods for the Pop-up for Adding Items

```
func alertForAddingItems(title: String,
                         placeholder: String)
    -> UIAlertController {
    let alertController = UIAlertController(title: title,
                                            message: nil,
                                            preferredStyle:
                                            .alert)
    alertController.addTextField { textField in
        textField.placeholder = placeholder
    }
    return alertController
}

func addActions(toAlertController alertController:
UIAlertController,
                saveActionHandler: @escaping ((UIAlertAction)
                -> Void))
    -> UIAlertController {
```

```
let saveAction = UIAlertAction(title: "Save", style:
.default, handler: saveActionHandler)
let cancelAction = UIAlertAction(title: "Cancel",
                                 style: .cancel,
                                 handler: { action in
                                     alertController.
                                     dismiss(animated: true,
                                     completion: nil)
                                 })

    alertController.addAction(saveAction)
    alertController.addAction(cancelAction)

    return alertController
}
```

That's everything you need in the ViewController. Now let's see the TasksViewController, which, as mentioned, will present the tasks for the list that was selected in the ViewController. In the viewDidLoad method, you need to load the tasks for the listName that was passed from the ViewController (Listing 3-5).

Listing 3-5. Loading Tasks for a List Name

```
override func viewDidLoad() {
        super.viewDidLoad()
        self.title = listName
        tasks =
        ListsManager.sharedInstance.tasksForList(withName:
        listName!)
}
```

The tasks array will provide the data to the table view. The table view data source and delegate methods are similar to the ones in the ViewController, so I will not explain them in greater detail (Listing 3-6).

The table view will support removing tasks by swiping from right to left. Tasks can be added with the add button in the navigation bar.

Listing 3-6. TasksViewController Implementation

```
func tableView(_ tableView: UITableView,
                numberOfRowsInSection section: Int) -> Int {
    return tasks.count
}

func tableView(_ tableView: UITableView,
               cellForRowAt indexPath: IndexPath)
-> UITableViewCell {
        var cell = tableView.dequeueReusableCell(withIdentifi
        er: cellIdentifier)
        if cell == nil {
            cell = UITableViewCell(style: .default,
            reuseIdentifier: cellIdentifier)
        }

        let taskName = tasks[indexPath.row]
        cell?.textLabel?.text = taskName

        return cell!
}

func tableView(_ tableView: UITableView,
               canEditRowAt indexPath: IndexPath) -> Bool {
    return true
}

func tableView(_ tableView: UITableView,
                      commit editingStyle:
                      UITableViewCellEditingStyle,
                      forRowAt indexPath: IndexPath) {
```

```
        if editingStyle == .delete {
            let name = tasks[indexPath.row]
            ListsManager.sharedInstance.finish(task: name)
            self.reloadTasks()
        }
    }

    @IBAction func addButtonClicked(sender: UIBarButtonItem) {
        let alertController = self.alertForAddingItems()
        self.present(alertController, animated: true,
        completion: nil)
    }

    private func alertForAddingItems() -> UIAlertController {
        let alertController = ListsSiriKit.alertForAddingItems(
                title: "Please provide task name",
                    placeholder: "Task name")
        return addActions(toAlertController: alertController,
                        saveActionHandler: { [unowned self]
                        action in
                            let textField = alertController.
                            textFields![0]
                            if let text = textField.text {
                                if text != "" {
                                    ListsManager.
                                    sharedInstance.add(tasks:
                                    [text],
                                     toList: self.listName!)
                                    self.reloadTasks()
                                }
                            }
                            alertController.dismiss(animated:
                            true, completion: nil)
```

```
                        })
   }

private func reloadTasks() {
        tasks =
        ListsManager.sharedInstance.tasksForList(withName:
        listName!)
        self.tableView.reloadData()
}
```

That's everything you need to do in the main iOS app. You can run it and add a few lists and tasks to it. Let's now start with the interesting part: implementing the Siri extension. As mentioned, you will need to implement protocols from three intents: INCreateTaskListIntent, INAddTasksIntent, and INSetTaskAttributeIntent. These intents are added in the Info. plist file of the Siri extension in the starter project. If you start from scratch, make sure you add them manually to the property list file.

INCreateTaskListIntent

The first protocol you need to implement is for handling the creation of lists. As you know already, the steps required to implement the SiriKit intent are confirm, resolve, and handle (the first two being optional). For this use case, you don't need the optional ones, so you will implement only the handle method. The handle method provides the intent, represented by the INCreateTaskListIntent object. This intent contains information about the title of the list that needs to be created, as well as any tasks that the user may have also provided in the request.

You should handle this request by providing an object of type INCreateTaskListIntentResponse in the completion handler of the method. INCreateTaskListIntentResponse also contains information about the title and the tasks, as well some additional things such as groupName, identifier, and created/modifiedDateComponents, which are not needed in this case. In the implementation provided in Listing 3-7, you first take the title of the intent and create the list using your ListsManager. Next, you check whether there are any tasks that need to be added to the list. If there are, you convert the strings provided by the intent to INTask objects, and you save the strings to your ListsManager. If everything goes OK, you send a successful response to the completion handler (Listing 3-7). The code in Listing 3-7 should be added as an extension to the IntentHandler. Put the code in the same file but not between the curly braces of the class definition of the IntentHandler. Instead, put it after it.

Listing 3-7. Implementing the INCreateTaskListIntent Object

```
extension IntentHandler : INCreateTaskListIntentHandling {

    public func handle(intent: INCreateTaskListIntent,
                                    completion: @escaping
(INCreateTaskListIntentResponse) -> Void) {
        guard let title = intent.title else {
            completion(INCreateTaskListIntentResponse(code:
            .failure, userActivity: nil))
            return
        }
        ListsManager.sharedInstance.createList(name: title.
        spokenPhrase)
        var tasks: [INTask] = []
        if let taskTitles = intent.taskTitles {
            let taskTitlesStrings = taskTitles.map {
                taskTitle -> String in
                return taskTitle.spokenPhrase
            }
            tasks = createTasks(fromTitles: taskTitlesStrings)
            ListsManager.sharedInstance.add(tasks:
            taskTitlesStrings, toList: title.spokenPhrase)
```

```
    }

    let response = INCreateTaskListIntentResponse(code:
    .success, userActivity: nil)
    response.createdTaskList = INTaskList(title: title,
                              tasks: tasks,
                              groupName: nil,
                              createdDateComponents: nil,
                              modifiedDateComponents: nil,
                              identifier: nil)
        completion(response)
    }
}
```

The method in Listing 3-7 uses a helper method called
createTasks(fromTitles:), which converts the task titles (which are
Strings) to the INTask objects that are needed for the response to Siri
(Listing 3-8). Add this method in the IntentHandler class (not in the
extension) since other extensions will also need it. The tasks have a status of
not completed since you are just creating them in a list. Updating the status
to completed will be done with the INSetTaskAttributeIntent object.

Listing 3-8. Converting Strings to INTask Objects

```
func createTasks(fromTitles taskTitles: [String]) -> [INTask] {
        var tasks: [INTask] = []
        tasks = taskTitles.map { taskTitle -> INTask in
            let task = INTask(title:
INSpeakableString(spokenPhrase: taskTitle),
                              status: .notCompleted,
                              taskType: .completable,
                              spatialEventTrigger: nil,
                              temporalEventTrigger: nil,
                              createdDateComponents: nil,
```

```
                          modifiedDateComponents: nil,
                          identifier: nil)
        return task
    }
    return tasks
}
```

Let's test this. One cool addition to Xcode 9 is that you can test Siri with the simulator (no more voice straining and disturbing everyone around you!). You can provide some sample text in the Siri scheme, and that command will be executed when you run the extension. Click the schemes button to the right of the Stop icon and then select "Manage schemes" and edit the Siri extension scheme. You will notice that in the Run action, there's a new input field called Siri Intent Query; that's the place where you should provide the text (Figure 3-7).

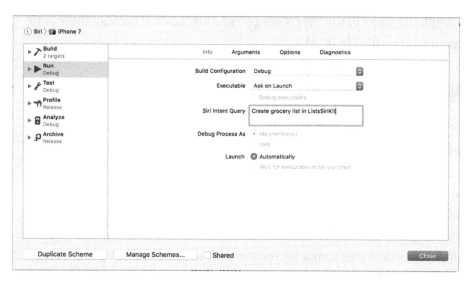

Figure 3-7. *Testing Siri on an iOS simulator*

After you run the Siri extension, you should see a confirmation from Siri that the list has been created (Figure 3-8).

75

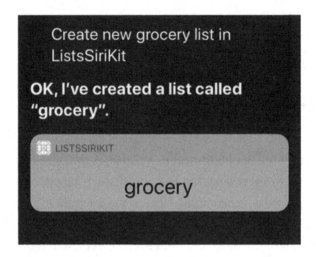

Figure 3-8. *Creating list in Siri*

Open the main app and verify that it also created the grocery list there. If it's not there, make sure your app groups are correctly configured, and go through the steps in the "App Groups" section again. That's all there is to creating lists with SiriKit!

INAddTasksIntent

Let's add some tasks to the list. To accomplish this, you need to implement the handle method of the INAddTasksIntentHandling protocol. You receive an INAddTasksIntent object, which similarly to INCreateTaskListIntent contains information about the task titles that need to be added, as well as the target list that will be modified. You can also provide spatial, which will display a reminder when the user approaches or leaves a specific location (or time, with a temporal event trigger). Just like you did with the creation of the list, you first extract the title of the list, and then you convert the task titles to INTask objects. You are adding the tasks to the ListsManager and provide a successful response if everything went fine during the process. Add the code in Listing 3-9 as a new extension to the IntentHandler class.

Listing 3-9. Adding Tasks to a List

```
extension IntentHandler : INAddTasksIntentHandling {
    public func handle(intent: INAddTasksIntent,
                       completion: @escaping
                       (INAddTasksIntentResponse)
-> Void) {
        let taskList = intent.targetTaskList
        guard let title = taskList?.title else {
            completion(INAddTasksIntentResponse(code: .failure,
            userActivity: nil))
            return
        }
        var tasks: [INTask] = []
        if let taskTitles = intent.taskTitles {
            let taskTitlesStrings = taskTitles.map {
                taskTitle -> String in
                return taskTitle.spokenPhrase
            }
            tasks = createTasks(fromTitles: taskTitlesStrings)
            ListsManager.sharedInstance.add(tasks:
            taskTitlesStrings, toList: title.spokenPhrase)
        }
        let response = INAddTasksIntentResponse(code: .success,
        userActivity: nil)
        response.modifiedTaskList = intent.targetTaskList
        response.addedTasks = tasks
        completion(response)
}
```

If you run the extension with text like "Add milk, sugar, and tomato in my grocery list in ListsSiriKit," you will get the Siri reply shown in Figure 3-9.

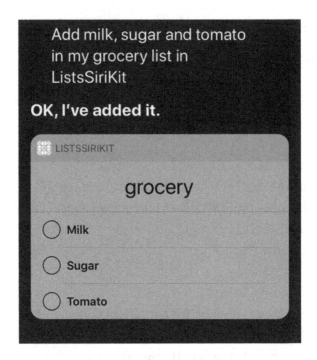

Figure 3-9. *Adding items to a list in Siri*

INSetTaskAttributeIntent

The last protocol you need to implement is
INSetTaskAttributeIntentHandling from INSetTaskAttributeIntent.
This protocol is used when you want to update the state of a task. A task in
SiriKit can be in three states: unknown, notCompleted, and completed. You
want to show the task in the list when it's in one of the first two states, but
when the task is completed, you want to remove it from the list. To do this,
you are extracting the title and status from the INSetTaskAttributeIntent
object. If the status is completed, you are just using the finish(task: title)
method from your ListsManager, which goes through the saved tasks and
deletes the completed task (Listing 3-10). Add the code in Listing 3-10 as
another extension to the IntentHandler class.

Listing 3-10. Setting Task Attributes Through Siri

```
extension IntentHandler : INSetTaskAttributeIntentHandling {

    public func handle(intent: INSetTaskAttributeIntent,
                       completion: @escaping
                       (INSetTaskAttributeIntentResponse) ->
                       Void) {

        guard let title = intent.targetTask?.title else {
            completion(INSetTaskAttributeIntentResponse(code:
            .failure, userActivity: nil))
            return
        }

        let status = intent.status

        if status == .completed {
            ListsManager.sharedInstance.finish(task: title.
            spokenPhrase)
        }
        let response = INSetTaskAttributeIntentResponse(code:
        .success, userActivity: nil)
        response.modifiedTask = intent.targetTask
        completion(response)
    }
}
```

If you tell Siri "Mark Sugar as completed in my grocery list in ListsSiriKit," it will give you something similar to Figure 3-10.

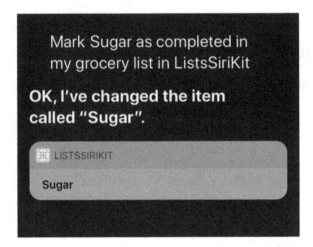

Figure 3-10. *Marking an item as completed*

If you open the main app, you will notice that the Sugar task is deleted from the grocery list, which is what you expected to happen. Now, let's see how you can verify this implementation with UI tests.

UI Testing with Siri

Testing is an essential step in verifying the quality of the software. It protects you from breaking functionalities while you are refactoring the code or adding new features. Smartly written tests can catch some edge-case bugs in the code. Although there are many benefits if you test your code, a lot of developers are still reluctant to write tests, mostly because of time constraints.

Here, you will concentrate on testing the Siri functionalities you have implemented in the lists app. While you were building the Siri integration for this app, you had to always give the phrase to Siri and then manually open the app and check whether the correct items were added. With UI testing, you will automate this step. There are other benefits too. Let's say your app supports many languages. To verify the integration in all the languages, you would need to perform several steps for every language.

1. Change the language on the device in Settings.

2. Check what the appropriate translation for the testing phrase is.

3. Learn how to pronounce this phrase.

4. Run Siri and provide the phrase.

5. Open the app to check whether the correct items were added.

6. Repeat these steps for every change that might have impact the Siri integration.

That is a lot of manual work, which can be simplified with UI testing. XCUISiriService provides the ability to activate expressions with voice recognition text, which can be taken from your Strings file for every language (or any other translation mechanism or format). The process can be fully automated and even connected with a continuous integration system, which can trigger the UI tests' execution on every commit.

Here you will test the creation of a list, as well as add items to the list. To get started, first you need to create a UI testing bundle, which you will call UITests (Figure 3-11).

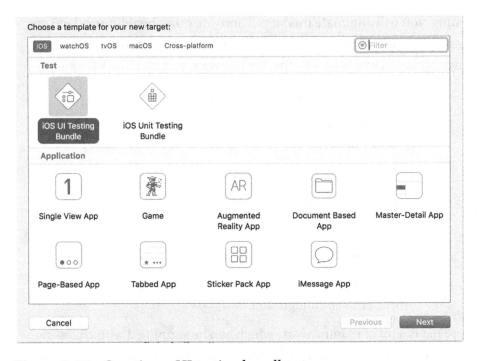

Figure 3-11. *Creating a UI testing bundle*

Next, create a subclass of `XCTestCase` and call it `SiriUITests`. Various tests tend to share a lot of common setup steps, tempting you to duplicate a lot of code. However, you will create a few helper methods, which will be used by all tests.

Start with the creation of a list with Siri. What should the test contain? First, you want to provide a test phrase for adding a list. Then, you want to automatically start the application (from the test) and check whether the table view that presents the created lists contains the list with the name you have provided in the test phrase. When you translate this into code, you get the test in Listing 3-11.

Listing 3-11. Testing the Creation of a List with Siri

```
func testCreatingList() {
    // Given
    let listName = "grocery"

    // Activate Siri
    let siri =
      self.siri(withExpression: "Create \(listName) list in
      ListsSiriKit")

    // Wait for Siri response
    waitForResponse(fromSiri: siri)

    // Launch the app
    let app = launchApp()

    // Check if grocery list exists
    testIfExists(item: listName, inApp: app)
}
```

In the method, you first define the list name that you are going to
create and then test whether it's present in the table view. Next, you
activate Siri with a standard expression for creating a list. Let's take a look
at this method (Listing 3-12).

Listing 3-12. Activating Siri

```
private func siri(withExpression expression: String)
-> XCUISiriService {
    let siri = XCUIDevice.shared.siriService
    siri.activate(voiceRecognitionText: expression)
    return siri
}
```

The method uses XCUISiriService, a new class introduced in iOS 11, which is used for activating Siri from UI tests. You return the created Siri service from this method since you will need it later in the test.

The test speaks the Siri expression, just like it would when you run it on a real device or when you set it from the scheme in the iOS simulator. This is why you have to wait until Siri responds to your expression. This is implemented in the method shown in Listing 3-13.

Listing 3-13. Waiting for the Siri Response

```
private func waitForResponse(
                 fromSiri siri: XCUISiriService) {
    let predicate = NSPredicate { (_, _) -> Bool in
        sleep(5)
        return true
    }
    let siriResponseExpectation =
            expectation(for: predicate,
                        evaluatedWith: siri,
                        handler: nil)
    self.wait(for: [siriResponseExpectation], timeout: 10)
}
```

You first define a predicate, which just sleeps for five seconds. Then, you create an expectation with that predicate, which will be evaluated with the Siri service you created in the previous method. Then you call the wait method, with the created expectation and a timeout of ten seconds. This means that after a delay of five seconds, you will be waiting for the Siri response for ten seconds.

Next, after Siri has (ideally) responded, you launch the application and check whether the new list has been created. The method in Listing 3-14 launches the app.

Listing 3-14. Launching the Test App

```
private func launchApp() -> XCUIApplication {
    let app = XCUIApplication()
    app.launch()
    return app
}
```

At this point while running the test, you will see the simulator starting your application. Now, let's check whether a new grocery list has been added to the table view. The next method takes a string as a parameter and checks whether that string is present in one of the cells of the table view that's currently displayed on the screen (Listing 3-15).

Listing 3-15. Testing Whether an Item Is Contained in the List

```
private func testIfExists(item: String, inApp app:
XCUIApplication) {
    let query = self.queryForItem(withName: item, inApp: app)
    XCTAssertTrue(query.count >= 1, "\(item) should exist")
}
```

To accomplish this, you use a helper method, which returns an object of type XCUIElementQuery. This object is used in UI tests for locating elements on the screen, which is what you need to verify the presence of the new element in the table view. These types of elements can be also chained with other queries. Let's see this helper method now (Listing 3-16).

Listing 3-16. Returning a Query for a Given Item Name

```
private func queryForItem(withName name: String,
                        inApp app: XCUIApplication)
-> XCUIElementQuery {
    let lists = app.tables.cells.staticTexts
```

```
    let query = lists.containing(.staticText, identifier: name)
    return query
}
```

Using the app object (which represents the started main iOS application), you take the tables that are currently present on the screen and afterward take all the cells in there with static text. This returns XCUIElementQuery, which you can then query to check whether it contains an item of type staticText (in the table view the grocery text will be presented in a static text label of a table view cell). You then return the query, and in an assert, you check whether it contains at least one element.

That's your first UI test for Siri. If you run it, you will see that it executes for about five to ten seconds. It starts the app, invokes Siri with the provided phrase, and then opens the app and checks whether the new item is there.

Next, you want to test whether the addition of items to the newly created list works properly. The test will be similar to what you have done so far, with some small changes and additions. First, in addition to the list name, you need to add a list of products to your Siri expression. Then, you invoke Siri as before and wait for the response. After that, you want to click the grocery list item and open the next screen, which presents a list of all the products added to the list. After you are on that screen, using the same approach for detecting whether an entry with the provided text exists, you will check whether "Milk" and "Sugar" are present in the list. At the end, you need to delete the newly added items to the list; otherwise, the list will grow with every new UI test (Listing 3-17).

Listing 3-17. Testing the Addition of Items to the List

```
func testAddingItems() {
    // Given
    let listName = "grocery"
    let products = [ "Milk", "Sugar" ]
    let productsPhrase = products.joined(separator: " and ")
```

```
let expression =
    "Add \(productsPhrase) in my \(listName) list in
    ListsSiriKit"

// Activate Siri
let siri = self.siri(withExpression: expression)

// Wait for Siri response
waitForResponse(fromSiri: siri)

// Launch the app
let app = launchApp()

// Select the grocery list
let query = self.queryForItem(withName: listName, inApp:
app)
query.element.tap()

// Check if milk exists
testIfExists(item: products[0], inApp: app)

// Check if sugar exists
testIfExists(item: products[1], inApp: app)

// Clear added items with the test
self.clear(items: products, listName: listName)
}
```

The method for clearing items takes a list of products and the list name as parameters and then goes through those items and calls a mark Siri command for all of them. If you remember, you have implemented the Mark intent (which is of type INSetTaskAttributeIntentHandling) by removing the item from the list. You have finished the task, and it doesn't need to be displayed in the list anymore (people who want to see visually how many tasks they have finished might disagree).

In the method (Listing 3-18), for every item you are doing part of the things you have already done in the tests, so you will reuse those methods. First, you create a marking expression for every item; then you create a new Siri service with that expression; finally, you wait for the Siri response. You can also reuse this same logic if you want to write tests for marking items.

Listing 3-18. Clearing the Added Items

```
private func clear(items: [String], listName: String) {
    for item in items {
        // Mark expression (will remove item from list)
        let expression =
            "Mark \(item) as completed in \(listName) list in
            ListsSiriKit"

        // Activate Siri for marking
        let markSiri = self.siri(withExpression: expression)

        // Wait for Siri response
        waitForResponse(fromSiri: markSiri)
    }
}
```

Now you have UI tests that can be automated to regularly check whether your integration with Siri works properly. This is a great feature of iOS 11, which ideally will be used by a lot of developers. With these example tests, you have the basis to start adding tests for your Siri-based apps.

Summary

That wraps up this chapter. The new Lists and Notes API opens up a lot of possibilities with different kinds of lists and notes, so you can get pretty creative here. To summarize, you implemented the three required protocols for creating lists, adding items to a list, and marking items as completed. Also, you enabled app groups to share the data between the main app and the Siri extension. At the end, you wrote UI tests to make sure your Siri integration works as expected.

CHAPTER 4

Speech, Synthesizers, and Dialogflow

At the same time SiriKit was announced, Apple also unveiled the Speech framework, the underlying voice recognition system that Siri uses. What does the Speech framework offer? It recognizes both live and prerecorded speech, creates transcriptions and alternative interpretations of the recognized text, and produces confidence levels of how accurate the transcription is. That sounds similar to what Siri does, so what's the difference between SiriKit and the Speech framework?

The Speech framework does only the speech-recognizing and the transcription parts. It's meant to be used inside your apps to get a user's input in a more efficient way than the standard method, which is typing on a keyboard. Users need to have the app launched in the foreground to start the recording and recognition of the speech, and you have to do this in a way that is transparent for the user. You will need to ask for permissions to access the speech recognition and the microphone but also make it clear to the user when you are recording. When your phone is locked or the app is in background, you can't start the recording by giving a voice command.

With SiriKit, on the other hand, the extensions that your app provides are available even from a locked phone. When the user says "Hey, Siri, book me a ride using YourCoolApp," Siri will recognize that your app needs to be asked to execute the request. Your app will get called (but not shown in the foreground) to handle the request, and Siri will provide the results to

© Martin Mitrevski 2018
M. Mitrevski, *Developing Conversational Interfaces for iOS*,
https://doi.org/10.1007/978-1-4842-3396-2_4

the user. This comes with some limitations, though. First, your app is never started; it just serves as a helper to Siri. Second, you can only help Siri in certain predefined domains, which I covered in the previous chapters. If the business case of your app doesn't fit in any of those domains, you can't use SiriKit.

Creating a Simple Grocery List

As discussed in Chapter 1, you can simplify the user experience by providing voice input to your apps. For example, let's say you have a to-do list or grocery list, similar to what you developed in Chapter 3. You want to be able to say something like "Add milk," which will add the product to your grocery list. After you buy the milk and therefore don't need it on the list anymore, you can say "Remove milk," which will remove it from the list. Let's see how you can implement this using the Speech framework.

The first part of this chapter will show how to add and remove predefined items to and from a grocery list. There won't be any fancy entity extraction with machine learning. You will do this in the final part of the chapter, when you will use a REST service (Dialogflow from Google) to add intelligence in your app. For now, you will just have a list of products that you expect to be added to the list. You will also define some removing words, such as delete and remove. When those words appear before a product, the product will be deleted from the list. In any other case, you will just add items to the list.

As mentioned, you can't start recording in a nontransparent way to the user. For this, you will have a button so the user can start the recording. The Speech framework might also access a web service to perform the speech recognition. This means that to remain free for every app, some limits are imposed by Apple for the service. Apple doesn't disclose how many requests you can do per day, but it warns you to be prepared to handle failures when this limit is hit. If you hit the limit too often, you should contact Apple to discuss this. The limit restriction is also enforced on the duration of the recording; Apple recommends no more than a minute. This means you can't just record all the time and wait for the user to start using it at some point; the service has to be turned on (on demand). Even though it's not explicitly stated, the Speech framework also works offline. You can test this by turning off the Internet on your device and saying something; you will see that it recognizes phrases locally.

In addition to the ability to click the button to stop the recording, you will allow the user to say something like "I'm done," which will stop the recording. This is pretty straightforward for implementation since the recording is already in progress, but you will need to see whether the transcribed text contains your defined stopping word or phrase.

Let's create a new single-view application and call it SpeechPlayground. There is a starter project that you can use to follow along. You will first add the needed permissions for accessing the feature in the Info.plist file. The permissions you need are "Privacy – Speech Recognition Usage Description" and "Privacy – Microphone Usage Description" (Figure 4-1).

Key	Type	Value
▼ Information Property List	Dictionary	(15 items)
Privacy - Speech Recognition Usage Description	String	Speech recognition needed for adding/removing items to the grocery list.
Privacy - Microphone Usage Description	String	Microphone needed for recording your voice when you want to add/remove
Localization native development region	String	en
Executable file	String	$(EXECUTABLE_NAME)

Figure 4-1. *Adding permissions in the property list*

Next, let's define a few products that you will support in the grocery list. Create a new products.json file and put some products in it (Listing 4-1).

Listing 4-1. Supported Products in the Grocery List

```
{
        "products": ["milk", "vegetables", "tomato", "fruit",
        "cucumber", "potato", "cheese", "orange"]
}
```

These will be the products that you will look for when you get a transcription from the Speech framework. Now let's dive into some coding. The first thing you need to do is check whether the user has granted you the permissions you need to access the speech-recognizing feature. If that's not the case, you will show an alert dialog (Listing 4-2). Call this method in the viewDidLoad method of the ViewController (the controller that will show the list of products and the recording functionality).

Listing 4-2. Checking Permissions for the Speech Framework in ViewController.swift

```
func checkPermissions() {
    var message: String? = nil
    SFSpeechRecognizer.requestAuthorization { (authStatus) in
        switch authStatus {
        case .denied:
            message = "Please enable access to speech recognition."
        case .restricted:
            message = "Speech recognition not available on this
            device."
        case .notDetermined:
            message = "Speech recognition is still not authorized."
        default: break
        }
        OperationQueue.main.addOperation() {
            self.recordingButton.isEnabled = authStatus ==
            .authorized
            if message != nil {
                self.showAlert(title: "Permissions error",
                message: message!)
            }
```

```
        }
    }
}
```

Next, you will add helper methods in the ViewController for the error messages that might appear because of permission errors or device limitations (Listing 4-3).

Listing 4-3. Helper Methods for Displaying Alerts

```
func showAlert(title: String, message: String) {
    let alert = UIAlertController(title: "Permissions error",
                                 message: message,
                                 preferredStyle: .alert)
    let action = UIAlertAction(title: "OK", style: .default,
    handler: nil)
    alert.addAction(action)
    self.present(alert, animated: true, completion: nil)
}

func showAudioError() {
    let errorTitle = "Audio Error"
    let errorMessage = "Recording is not possible at the moment."
    self.showAlert(title: errorTitle, message: errorMessage)
}
```

This is standard code for showing an alert on iOS, using the UIAlertController. You just define an OK action and add it to the alert controller. This action will be presented to the user, reminding them that they haven't provided the required permissions to perform the recording.

Tip For real production apps, it's always a good idea to extract your words in a separate strings file and access them in the code by their keys. It will make your life a lot easier, especially when you have a lot of words that are repeating throughout the app and also when you need to support different languages.

You will need a class called SpeechHelper, which will return the keywords that you need to recognize—the products, the stopping words, and the removal words. I've extracted this in a separate class to isolate the loading of the words. Currently they are hard-coded words, but they can easily be retrieved from a web service, without changing the main code (Listing 4-4).

Listing 4-4. SpeechHelper Class Implementation

```
class SpeechHelper: NSObject {
    class func loadProducts() -> Set<String> {
        var products = Set<String>()
        let fileUrl = Bundle.main.url(forResource: "products",
                                withExtension: "json")
        do {
            let jsonData = try Data(contentsOf: fileUrl!)
            let json = try JSONSerialization.jsonObject(with:
            jsonData, options: .allowFragments)
                as! [String: Array<String>]
            if let loadedProducts = json["products"] {
                for product in loadedProducts {
                    products.insert(product)
                }
            }
```

```
    } catch {
        print("error loading products")
    }
    return products
}

class func removalWords() -> Set<String> {
    return ["delete", "erase", "remove"]
}

class func stoppingWords() -> Set<String> {
    return ["stop", "done"]
}
}
```

There's nothing special in the previous chunk of code; you just load the products from the products.json file you created earlier and define words for removing products and stopping the recording. Let's see how you will use these methods in the ViewController. You will define three arrays of Strings (removalWords, stoppingWords, and products), which will be populated with the data from the SpeechHelper in the viewDidLoad method (Listing 4-5).

Listing 4-5. Loading Words from the SpeechHelper in the ViewController

```
func setupRemovalWords() {
        removalWords = SpeechHelper.removalWords()
}

func setupStoppingWords() {
        stoppingWords = SpeechHelper.stoppingWords()
}
```

```swift
func loadProducts() {
        products = SpeechHelper.loadProducts()
}

override func viewDidLoad() {
        super.viewDidLoad()
        loadProducts()
        setupRemovalWords()
        setupStoppingWords()
        checkPermissions()
        speechRecognizer.delegate = self
}
```

Now, let's start with the interesting part. The user interface (already provided in the sample project) will be pretty simple—there will be a button through which you will trigger the start/stop of the recording, a text view that will show what the Speech framework transcribed for you, and a table view that will list the products you need to buy (Figure 4-2).

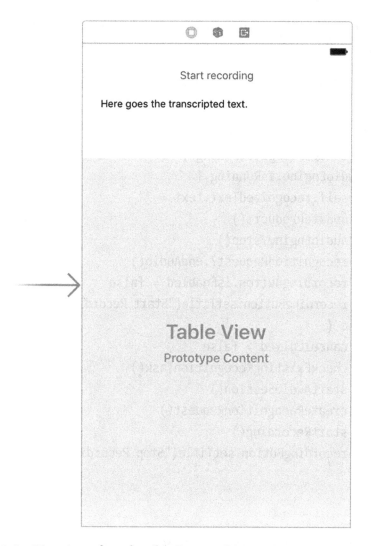

Figure 4-2. *User interface for the GroceryList app*

You need to add an IBAction to the recording button in the
ViewController, which will call the handleRecordingStateChange
method. This method will check the state of the audio session, and based
on that, it will either start or stop the recording session (Listing 4-6).

Listing 4-6. Handling the State Change of a Recording in the ViewController

```swift
@IBAction func startRecording(sender: UIButton) {
        handleRecordingStateChange()
}

func handleRecordingStateChange() {
    if audioEngine.isRunning {
        self.recognizedText.text = ""
        updateProducts()
        audioEngine.stop()
        recognitionRequest?.endAudio()
        recordingButton.isEnabled = false
        recordingButton.setTitle("Start Recording", for: .normal)
    } else {
        cancelCalled = false
        checkExistingRecognitionTask()
        startAudioSession()
        createRecognitionRequest()
        startRecording()
        recordingButton.setTitle("Stop Recording", for: .normal)
    }
}
```

Implementing Speech Recognition

So you understand this method and its two states, I will introduce a few new types of objects (variables in the ViewController are provided in the starter project). I will start with the audioEngine variable. It's an object from the class AVAudioEngine, which contains a group of nodes (AVAudioNodes). These nodes perform the job of audio signal creation, processing, and I/O tasks. Without these nodes, the engine wouldn't be able to do its job, but also AVAudioNodes does not currently provide useful functionality until attached to an engine. You can create your own AVAudioNodes object and attach it to the engine, using the attach(_ node: AVAudioNode) method.

Let's introduce another new object, recognitionRequest, of the class SFSpeechAudioBufferRecognitionRequest. This class is used for requests that recognize live audio or in-memory content, which is what you need in this case. You want to show and update the transcribed text when the user says something.

The third object I will introduce is recognitionTask (SFSpeechRecognitionTask). With this task, you can monitor the recognition process. The task can be either starting, running, finishing, canceling, or completed. This kind of object is what you get when you ask the speech recognizer to start listening to the user input and return what it heard to you. The speech recognizer is represented by the SFSpeechRecognizer class, which is the class that does the actual speech recognizing. You may have noticed that you have set the ViewController to be the delegate of the speech recognizer in the viewDidLoad method. It supports only one language and using the default initializer returns a speech recognizer for the device's current locale (if a recognizer is supported for that locale). If you want to be sure that English transcription will be used, you can create the speech recognizer by explicitly stating its locale (Listing 4-7).

Listing 4-7. Creating the Speech Recognizer with an English Locale

```
private let speechRecognizer: SFSpeechRecognizer! =
        SFSpeechRecognizer(locale: Locale.init(identifier:
        "en-US"))
```

You just learned about a lot of new classes; let's see how you can put them all together. With the isRunning method of the audioEngine, you are checking whether there's an audio session in progress at the moment. If there's no such session, you do several things (you can ignore

101

the cancelCalled flag for now; I will get back to it later). First, you check whether you already have a recognition task that is in progress. If there is, you will just cancel it and nil it out (Listing 4-8).

Listing 4-8. Checking for Existing Recognition Tasks

```
func checkExistingRecognitionTask() {
        if recognitionTask != nil {
            recognitionTask?.cancel()
            recognitionTask = nil
        }
}
```

Next, you start the audio session (Listing 4-9). You set the category of the session to be AVAudioSessionCategoryRecord, which only records the session. If you want to also play it later, you should use AVAudioSessionCategoryPlayAndRecord. Next, you set the mode of the session to AVAudioSessionModeMeasurement. Apple recommends you use this mode if your app is handling audio input or output because it does minimal signal processing on the audio.

Listing 4-9. Starting the Audio Session

```
func startAudioSession() {
   let audioSession = AVAudioSession.sharedInstance()
   do {
       try audioSession.setCategory(AVAudioSessionCategoryRecord)
       try audioSession.setMode(AVAudioSessionModeMeasurement)
       try audioSession.setActive(true, with:
.notifyOthersOnDeactivation)
   } catch {
       showAudioError()
   }
}
```

After starting the session, you create the recognition request (Listing 4-10). Note that you set shouldReportPartialResults to true, which means that the task will report the progress all the time, not only when the recording finishes. This enables you to show (and update) the text view, which will hold the text on each new spoken word.

Listing 4-10. Creating the Recognition Request

```
func createRecognitionRequest() {
    recognitionRequest = SFSpeechAudioBufferRecognitionRequest()
    recognitionRequest?.shouldReportPartialResults = true
}
```

Finally, you can start recording. The method shown in Listing 4-11 does that.

Listing 4-11. Starting the Recording

```
func startRecording() {
    guard let inputNode = audioEngine.inputNode else {
        showAudioError()
        return
    }
    recognitionTask = speechRecognizer.recognitionTask(
                                        with:
                                        recognitionRequest!,
                                        resultHandler:{
        [unowned self] (result, error) in
        var recognized: String?
        self.createProductsArraysForSession()
        if result != nil {
            var shouldDelete = false
```

```
            recognized = result?.bestTranscription.
            formattedString
            for segment in (result?.bestTranscription.
            segments)! {
                let text = segment.substring.lowercased()
                if self.removalWords.contains(text) {
                    shouldDelete = true
                }
                if self.checkStoppingWords(text: text) == true {
                    return
                }
                if self.products.contains(text) {
                    if (shouldDelete == false) {
                        self.sessionProducts.append(text)
                    } else {
                        self.deletedProducts.append(text)
                    }
                    shouldDelete = false
                }
            }
            self.recognizedText.text = recognized
        }
        var finishedRecording = false
        if result != nil {
            finishedRecording = result!.isFinal
        }
        if error != nil || finishedRecording {
            inputNode.removeTap(onBus: 0)
            self.handleFinishedRecording()
        }
    })
```

```
let recordingFormat = inputNode.outputFormat(forBus: 0)
inputNode.installTap(onBus: 0, bufferSize: 1024, format:
recordingFormat) {
    [unowned self] (buffer, when) in
    self.recognitionRequest?.append(buffer)
}
startAudioEngine()
}
```

Several things are going on here, but as you will see, this method is not that complicated. First, you check whether there's an inputNode available for the engine and show an error if there isn't. Then, you start the recognition task for the speech recognizer, with the recognition request you created. I will get back to the resultHandler later; here, you will see how to start the audio engine. You do this by first installing an audio tap on the bus of the input node, with a buffer size of 1,024 bytes. Then you try to start the audio engine, by first pre-allocating many of the resources the engine requires with the prepare method and by then starting the engine with the start method (Listing 4-12).

Listing 4-12. Starting the Audio Engine

```
func startAudioEngine() {
      audioEngine.prepare()
      do {
          try audioEngine.start()
      } catch {
          showAudioError()
      }
}
```

Now let's examine the result handler. You are initializing two arrays (the createProductsArraysForSession method in Listing 4-13) that you need for keeping track of which products you want to add and remove from the grocery list.

Listing 4-13. Creating Session Arrays

```
func createProductsArraysForSession() {
        self.sessionProducts = [String]()
        self.deletedProducts = [String]()
}
```

When there's a result in the resultHandler of the speech recognition task, you get the best transcription by calling result?.bestTranscription.formattedString. If you want to show a pop-up with other transcriptions and let the user choose the one that fits best, you can call result?.transcriptions, which will give you an array of the possible transcriptions.

Every SFTranscription object contains two properties: formattedString and segments (SFTranscriptionSegment). Segments contain other information that you might find helpful, such as confidence (on a scale of 0 to 1), which indicates how sure the Speech framework is that this string is the one the user has spoken. This property is used when figuring out which transcription is bestTranscription.

You use the segments array of the best transcription (result?.bestTranscription.segments) to iterate through all the spoken words. First, you check whether there's a removal word (*remove* or *delete*) before a given word (self.removalWords.contains(text)). You track this with the shouldDelete flag. If the flag is set, you add the word to the deletedProducts array. Otherwise, it goes to the sessionProducts array (it's a new product that the user has spoken). You also check whether the word is a stopping one (self.checkStoppingWords(text: text)). If it is, you just return from the method.

As mentioned previously, you want to write and update the transcription as the user gives voice commands. That's why you are setting the recognized text to your text view (`self.recognizedText.text = recognized`). Then you check whether the recording finished (`finishedRecording = result!.isFinal`). If it is, you remove the audio tap from the input node's bus, which you added at the beginning; then you nil out the request and the task and stop the audio engine.

Now let's go back to the `cancelCalled` flag. It is used to stop subsequent calls to the method that updates everything when the recording state changes (`handleRecordingStateChange`). The subsequent calls can happen because the result handler is called on every sound that's recognized, which means it can be called even after the triggering stop word is found. The flag is used in the method that checks for stopping words (Listing 4-14).

Listing 4-14. Checking for Words That Stop the Recording

```
func checkStoppingWords(text: String) -> Bool {
    if self.stoppingWords.contains(text) {
        if self.cancelCalled == false {
            self.handleRecordingStateChange()
            self.cancelCalled = true
            return true
        }
    }
    return false
}
```

I've covered everything you need to do when the session is not currently running and you have to start it. Now, let's see the other state—when you have a recording that you need to stop and update the list based on the transcription. As a quick refresher, please check Listing 4-6 again, before proceeding with the explanation of the methods in the running state of the audio engine.

The first method you call in the running state of the
handleRecordingStateChange method is updateProducts (Listing 4-15),
which first stores the currently displayed products in a temporary variable.
Then it adds the ones that should be added in the current session. After
that, it goes through all the products and checks whether they are in the
deleted products list. This means that your current logic will delete all
occurrences of an item of the list if the remove word is found before it.

Listing 4-15. Updating Products After the Recording Is Finished

```swift
func updateProducts() {
    var tmp = addedProducts
    tmp.append(contentsOf: sessionProducts)
    addedProducts = [String]()
    for product in tmp {
        if !deletedProducts.contains(product) {
            addedProducts.append(product)
        }
    }
    self.productsTableView.reloadData()
}
```

Apart from updating the products, you also need to stop the
audio engine, end the recognition request, and update the state of the
recording button.

There is a possibility that while the app is running, the speech
recognizer becomes unavailable for some reason. That's why you set
the delegate of the speech recognizer to be the ViewController. In the
implementation, you are setting the availability of the recording button
based on this state change (Listing 4-16).

Listing 4-16. Handling Availability Change of the Recongizer

```
func speechRecognizer(_ speechRecognizer: SFSpeechRecognizer,
                      availabilityDidChange available: Bool)
{
    if available {
        recordingButton.isEnabled = true
    } else {
        recordingButton.isEnabled = false
    }
}
```

The last pieces of code not covered yet are the UITableViewDataSource methods (Listing 4-17). They contain a standard implementation for displaying contents of a data source (in your case the addedProducts array).

Listing 4-17. Table View Data Source Implementation

```
func tableView(_ tableView: UITableView,
                     cellForRowAt  indexPath: IndexPath) ->
                     UITableViewCell {
    var cell: UITableViewCell? =
        tableView.dequeueReusableCell(withIdentifier:
        "ProductCell")
    if cell == nil {
        cell = UITableViewCell(style: .default,
                                            reuseIdentifier:
                                            "ProductCell")
    }
    cell?.textLabel?.text = addedProducts[indexPath.row]
    return cell!
}
```

```
func tableView(_ tableView: UITableView,
                    numberOfRowsInSection section: Int) ->
                    Int {
    return addedProducts.count
}
```

You can test this by providing sample phrases. The end result should look like Figure 4-3.

Figure 4-3. *Adding items to the grocery list*

Implementing Text to Speech

You saw in the previous section how an iOS device can understand and transcribe the voice commands you give to it (speech to text). Now, you will see the opposite—how the device can communicate information you have as a string in your app, with speech. You will extend the GroceryList app by adding functionality that tells the user what remaining products they need to buy from the list. You will also provide a way to customize the voice that will do the speaking, through a Settings page. Users will be able to change the language of the speaker, the voice pitch, the speaking rate, the volume, and the delay.

Using AVSpeechSynthesizer

To get started with this part, make sure you have completed the previous part. If you had trouble doing that, continue with the already completed sample project from the previous section. To add text to speech to your GroceryList app, you will need a different class (AVSpeechSynthesizer) from a different framework (AVFoundation). This class produces synthesized speech from text on an iOS device and provides methods for controlling or monitoring the progress of ongoing speech, which is exactly what you need.

Let's first create an object from this class. There's also a new variable for the audioSession since you will use it in more methods and you don't want to always call the sharedInstance class method (Listing 4-18).

Listing 4-18. Adding Variables for Speech Synthesizing and Audio Sessions

```
private var speechSynthesizer = AVSpeechSynthesizer()
private var audioSession = AVAudioSession.sharedInstance()
```

For the class to be able to speak your text, you need to provide it with an object of type AVSpeechUtterance. An AVSpeechUtterance object is the basic part of speech synthesis. It keeps information about the text that will be spoken and parameters that can customize the voice, pitch, rate, and delay. The speech synthesizer keeps a queue (FIFO data structure) of utterances to be spoken. There's a method that checks whether the synthesizer is currently speaking, and if it does, it just adds the next utterances to the queue. It also provides methods to pause, play, and stop the speech, which might be useful if you want to develop an audio book app.

You will persist the user preferences about the speech parameters between app launches, and for this you will create a new class—SettingsManager. The class provides methods for saving and getting the values for the speech parameters (Listing 4-19).

Listing 4-19. The SettingsManager Class

```swift
class SettingsManager: NSObject {

    static let volumeKey = "volume"
    static let pitchKey = "pitch"
    static let delayKey = "delay"
    static let rateKey = "rate"
    static let languageKey = "language"

    class func currentVolume() -> Float {
        return self.valueFor(key: volumeKey, defaultValue:
        Float(0.9)) as! Float
    }

    class func setVolume(value: Float) {
        self.set(value: value, key: volumeKey)
    }

    class func currentPitch() -> Float {
        return self.valueFor(key: pitchKey, defaultValue:
        Float(1)) as! Float
    }

    class func setPitch(value: Float) {
        self.set(value: value, key: pitchKey)
    }

    class func currentDelay() -> Double {
        return self.valueFor(key: delayKey, defaultValue: 0.0)
        as! Double
    }

    class func setDelay(value: Double) {
        self.set(value: value, key: delayKey)
    }
```

```swift
class func currentRate() -> Float {
    return self.valueFor(key: rateKey, defaultValue:
    Float(0.5)) as! Float
}

class func setRate(value: Float) {
    self.set(value: value, key: rateKey)
}

class func languageCode() -> String {
    return self.valueFor(key: languageKey, defaultValue:
    "en-US") as! String
}

class func setLanguageCode(value: String) {
    self.set(value: value, key: languageKey)
}

class private func valueFor(key: String, defaultValue: Any)
-> Any {
    if let value = UserDefaults.standard.value(forKey: key) {
        return value
    }
    return defaultValue
}

class private func set(value: Any, key: String) {
    UserDefaults.standard.set(value, forKey: key)
    UserDefaults.standard.synchronize()
}
}
```

Now, let's extend your storyboard with new screens and design updates (Figures 4-4 and 4-5).

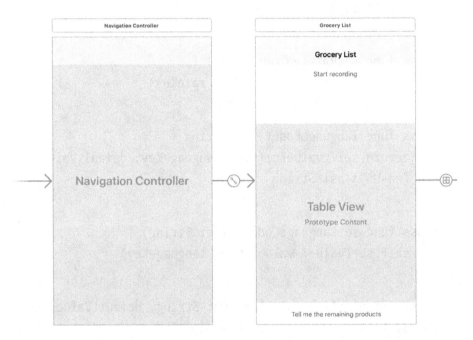

Figure 4-4. *Extending the grocery list storyboard with a navigation controller*

You changed the root view controller to be UINavigationViewController to be able to push view controllers from the initial grocery list screen. On the grocery list screen, there are two new buttons: Settings (which will open the Settings screen and the ShowSettings segue) and "Tell me the remaining products," which will invoke the text-to-speech feature. There's another screen that is opened from the Settings screen, LanguageViewController. It will show a list of the available languages that can be used in the speech utterance.

The SettingsViewController is pretty simple; it has four sliders for the parameters needed to customize the voice and a button that will show the language selection (Figure 4-5). The sliders' maximum and minimum values are set in Interface Builder, based on Apple's documentation for the possible values. The volume and rate sliders have possible float values from 0 to 1, the pitching has values from 0.5 to 2, and for the delay I've set a limit of 5 seconds. The values in the sliders are read from the SettingsManager you saw earlier (Listing 4-20).

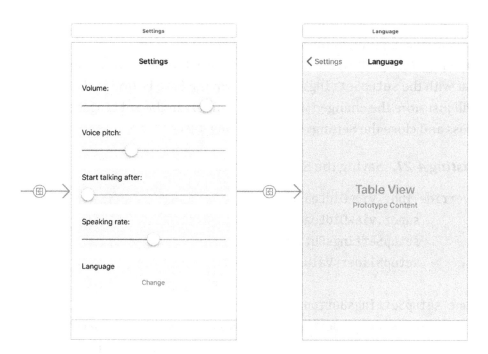

Figure 4-5. *SettingsViewController and LanguageViewController*

Listing 4-20. Setting the Values in the Sliders in SettingsViewController

```
@IBOutlet weak var volumeSlider: UISlider!
@IBOutlet weak var pitchSlider: UISlider!
@IBOutlet weak var delaySlider: UISlider!
@IBOutlet weak var rateSlider: UISlider!
```

115

```
func setupSlidersValues() {
    volumeSlider.value = SettingsManager.currentVolume()
    pitchSlider.value = SettingsManager.currentPitch()
    delaySlider.value = Float(SettingsManager.currentDelay())
    rateSlider.value = SettingsManager.currentRate()
}
```

Call this method in the `viewDidLoad` method of the `SettingsViewController`. Also, add the Save button in the navigation bar with the `setupSettingsButton`. When the Save button is clicked, you will just store the changed values of the sliders in the `SettingsManager` class and close the Settings screen (Listing 4-21).

Listing 4-21. Saving the Sliders' Values

```
override func viewDidLoad() {
        super.viewDidLoad()
        setupSettingsButton()
        setupSlidersValues()
}
func setupSettingsButton() {
        let settingsButton = UIBarButtonItem(title: "Save",
                                             style: .plain,
                                             target: self,
                                             action:
#selector(saveButtonClicked))
        self.navigationItem.rightBarButtonItem = settingsButton
}
func saveButtonClicked() {
    SettingsManager.setVolume(value: volumeSlider.value)
    SettingsManager.setPitch(value: pitchSlider.value)
    SettingsManager.setDelay(value: Double(delaySlider.value))
```

```
SettingsManager.setRate(value: rateSlider.value)
_ = self.navigationController?.popViewController(animated:
true)
}
```

When the Change button is tapped, the LanguageViewController is shown, by performing the ShowLanguage segue (Listing 4-22).

Listing 4-22. Showing the LanguageViewController

```
@IBAction func changeLanguageClicked(sender: UIButton) {
      self.performSegue(withIdentifier: "ShowLanguages",
      sender: self)
   }
```

The LanguageViewController gets the available voice languages from the AVSpeechSynthesisVoice class and displays them in a table view. When a row is selected, the check mark is set to the selected row, and the table view is reloaded (Listing 4-23).

Listing 4-23. LanguageViewController Implementation

```
class LanguageViewController: UIViewController,
UITableViewDataSource, UITableViewDelegate {
    var languages: [String] = [String]()
    var selectedLanguage: String!

    override func viewDidLoad() {
        super.viewDidLoad()

        selectedLanguage = SettingsManager.languageCode()
        languages = Array(Set(AVSpeechSynthesisVoice.
        speechVoices().map {
 return $0.language }))
    }
```

```swift
func tableView(_ tableView: UITableView,
            cellForRowAt indexPath: IndexPath) ->
            UITableViewCell {
    var cell: UITableViewCell? =
        tableView.dequeueReusableCell(withIdentifier:
        "ProductCell")
    if cell == nil {
        cell = UITableViewCell(style: .default,
                                reuseIdentifier:
                                "ProductCell")
    }
    let current = languages[indexPath.row]
    cell?.textLabel?.text = current
    cell?.accessoryType =
            current == selectedLanguage ? .checkmark : .none
    return cell!
}

func tableView(_ tableView: UITableView,
            numberOfRowsInSection section: Int) -> Int {
    return languages.count
}

func tableView(_ tableView: UITableView,
            didSelectRowAt indexPath: IndexPath) {
    tableView.deselectRow(at: indexPath, animated: true)
    selectedLanguage = languages[indexPath.row]
    SettingsManager.setLanguageCode(value:
    selectedLanguage)
    tableView.reloadData()
}
}
```

Let's go back to the grocery list screen, the `ViewController`. You need to provide an implementation for the method that is called when the "Tell me the remaining products" button is tapped (Listing 4-24). In this method, you first check whether the speech synthesizer is currently speaking. If it is, you will just let it continue doing that. Otherwise, you call the speak method, with a newly created utterance.

Listing 4-24. Playing the Remaining Text

```
@IBAction func remainingProducts(sender: UIButton) {
        playRemainingText()
}

func playRemainingText() {
   if speechSynthesizer.isSpeaking {
      speechSynthesizer.continueSpeaking()
   } else {
      speechSynthesizer.speak(self.createUtterance())
   }
}
```

The `createUtterance` method creates the utterance by reading the parameters the user has set on the Settings screen for rate, pitch multiplier, volume, delay, and voice (Listing 4-25).

Listing 4-25. Creating Utterance from the SettingsManager Values

```
func createUtterance() -> AVSpeechUtterance {
   let text = createRemainingText()
   let speechUtterance = AVSpeechUtterance(string: text)
   speechUtterance.rate = SettingsManager.currentRate()
   speechUtterance.pitchMultiplier = SettingsManager.
   currentPitch()
   speechUtterance.volume = SettingsManager.currentVolume()
```

```
speechUtterance.preUtteranceDelay = SettingsManager.
currentDelay()
speechUtterance.voice =
    AVSpeechSynthesisVoice(language: SettingsManager.
    languageCode())
return speechUtterance
}
```

The text that will be spoken is created in the createRemainingText, which goes through the addedProducts list and adds the items to the text (Listing 4-26). You use commas to separate the words since the synthesizer takes this into consideration and pronounces them in a more natural way. Without a comma, it will just rush through the items. If the user has an empty grocery list, you will change the text to a message that informs them that there are no remaining products in the list.

Listing 4-26. Creating the Text That Will Be Read to the User

```
func createRemainingText() -> String {
    var text = "You need to buy the following products: "
    if addedProducts.count > 0 {
        for product in addedProducts {
            text += product
            text += ","
        }
        text += "."
    } else {
        text = "You don't have remaining products on your
        grocery list."
    }
    return text
}
```

Before running the app, make sure to add the Settings button in the navigation bar. When this button is tapped, it will show the Settings screen you created earlier (Listing 4-27). You need to call the setupSettingsButton in the viewDidLoad method of the ViewController.

Listing 4-27. Setting Up the Settings Button

```
func setupSettingsButton() {
        let settingsButton = UIBarButtonItem(title: "Settings",
                                             style: .plain,
                                             target: self,
                                             action: #selector
(settingsButtonClicked))
        self.navigationItem.rightBarButtonItem = settingsButton
}

func settingsButtonClicked() {
        self.performSegue(withIdentifier: "ShowSettings",
        sender: self)
}
```

If you run the app and tap the remaining button first, you will hear a voice saying "You don't have any remaining products on your grocery list." That's great; it's what you expect. Now let's add some products with the recording and speech recognizing you've implemented in the previous project. When you tap the remaining button again, nothing happens. What seems to be the problem, and why did it stop working? Somehow after the recording, the device doesn't have the ability to play a sound.

That's exactly what happens. When I was discussing the startAudioSession method in the previous section, I said that the category of the audio session is AVAudioSessionCategoryRecord. That was good enough for you then, but now you have a new feature, which requires playing sound. That's why you will change the category to be AVAudioSessionCategoryPlayAndRecord (Listing 4-28).

Listing 4-28. Changing the Category of the AVAudioSession

```
func startAudioSession() {
    do {
        try audioSession.setCategory(AVAudioSessionCategoryPlay
        AndRecord)
        try audioSession.setMode(AVAudioSessionModeMeasurement)
        try audioSession.setActive(true,
                                    with:
                                    .notifyOthersOnDeactivation)
    } catch {
        showAudioError()
    }
}
```

Another improvement you can make to your grocery list is to get rid of the stopping words. You don't want to always say "I'm done." The recorder should be smart enough to stop the recording when there's no action for some time. Since the Speech framework currently doesn't provide this functionality, you can implement this by yourself. You can use a timer, which will be re-created on every call to the result handler of the speech recognition task. If a timer manages to live for two seconds (long enough for the method that's scheduled to be invoked), the recording will be stopped. Replace the creation of the recognition task in the startRecording method with the code in Listing 4-29.

Listing 4-29. Updating the Recognition Task with a Timer That Stops the Recording

```
recognitionTask = speechRecognizer.recognitionTask(
    with: recognitionRequest!,
    resultHandler: { [unowned self] (result, error) in
        var recognized: String?
```

```
self.createProductsArraysForSession()
if result != nil {
    var shouldDelete = false
    recognized = result?.bestTranscription.
    formattedString
    for segment in (result?.bestTranscription.
    segments)! {
        let text = segment.substring.lowercased()
        if self.removalWords.contains(text) {
            shouldDelete = true
        }
        if self.products.contains(text) {
            if (!shouldDelete) {
                self.sessionProducts.append(text)
            } else {
                self.deletedProducts.append(text)
            }
            shouldDelete = false
        }
        self.timer?.invalidate()
        self.timer = nil
        if !self.cancelCalled {
            self.timer = Timer.scheduledTimer(withT
            imeInterval: 2,
                                    repeats: false,
                                    block: { _ in
                            _ = self.handleStop()
            })
        }
    }
    self.recognizedText.text = recognized
}
```

```
        var finishedRecording = false
        if result != nil {
            finishedRecording = result!.isFinal
        }
        if error != nil || finishedRecording {
            inputNode.removeTap(onBus: 0)
            self.handleFinishedRecording()
        }
    })
```

That's the last detail you needed to do. You can now add products and play with the voice parameters (hint: the pitch parameter might be fun). You now have two directional speech communications, from speech to text and vice versa.

Using Dialogflow (api.ai)

Dialogflow (formerly known as api.ai) is a conversational user experience platform, recently acquired by Google. It uses natural language processing and machine learning algorithms to extract entities and actions from text. The best thing about it is that it has a web application through which you can train your intents with custom sentences. Based on that, you get a JSON response with the recognized data. This brings a whole new set of opportunities for developers since natural language processing and machine learning are not trivial tasks—a lot of expertise and research in this area are required to get it right. On top of that, the service is currently free for developers. As you will see, Dialogflow offers a lot of powerful features, and it's definitely worth a look.

You will extend the grocery list app you were developing in the previous two sections. Make sure you have the previous two projects completed before moving on. If you struggled with those, please start with the completed project from the previous section. One thing you did very naively in those two apps was to extract the words in a sentence—this was done by plain string matching with hard-coded predefined words in your app. It didn't take into consideration the context in which the keywords were spoken. For example, if you said something like "I don't need chicken anymore," it will still add chicken to the list, although it's clear that you have to remove it. Let's solve these issues and put some intelligence in your app by using Dialogflow.

To get started with Dialogflow, you need to sign up with a Google account and then create an agent. You will create one called GroceryList (Figure 4-6).

Figure 4-6. *Creating an agent in Dialogflow*

Training a Dialogflow Agent

An *agent* is a container for a group of actions that you build with intents. You can define multiple intents for an action. An *intent* is, simply put, what the user says. It can contain entities, which are the objects you want to be recognized in the sentence. You can define your own entities or use the ones provided by the system. `Chicken` is an entity of your type `Product` in the earlier sentence. It might look a bit abstract at the moment, but it will all make sense when you look at the examples. The developer documentation can also be helpful to better understand these concepts.

Now let's create the product entity and add some values there. One cool thing is that you can also define synonyms of the words you've provided. After you create the entity, you can always update the list with new values, and that's already a lot better than your current implementation (Figure 4-7).

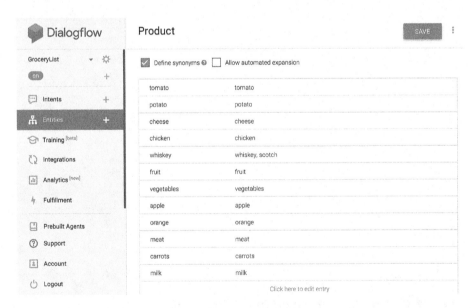

Figure 4-7. *Adding values to the Product entity*

Now let's add intents. In this use case, the user can have two intents—either add something to the list or remove it. You will create two separate intents for these, but you will also have in mind cases where the user had two intents in one sentence—to both add and remove something.

First, you create the AddProduct intent. You add the product.add action there and create two parameters for it. As I mentioned, you want to handle two possible intents in a sentence, and that's why you need the two parameters. The first one is called AddProduct; it's an entity of the type Product you just created. It's mandatory (there has to be a product in an AddProduct intent), and it can be also a list (the users can provide as many values as they want in a sentence). You can also define a prompt. This is like an additional question that the platform will return in case a mandatory value is missing (Figure 4-8).

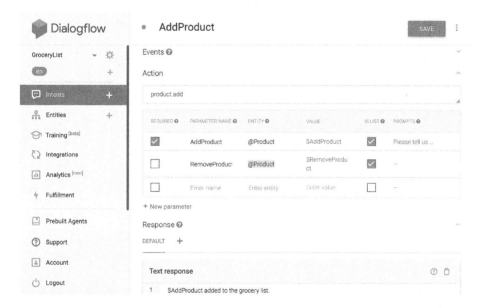

Figure 4-8. *Creating an AddProduct intent and defining mandatory and optional entities for it*

127

The second parameter that you have defined is RemoveProduct, which is also an entity of type Product, and it can be a list. This one is optional for the Add action; the users don't have to remove something if they want to add products to the list. However, this parameter will be mandatory for the product.remove action.

You can also define a text response for your action. This is useful for testing, as you will see, and it's also included in the JSON response if you want to show it in your apps.

Now let's add some sentences to the intent. These are samples of what the user might say, and with every new entry, the model is re-trained and becomes more precise when it encounters a new sentence. When you add sentences, you train the model by specifying which part of the sentence is which parameter. Over time, the model will find those parameters by itself, which is pretty cool and gives a glimpse of the huge power of machine learning. The AddProduct parameters are labeled in orange, and the RemoveProduct parameters are yellow (Figure 4-9).

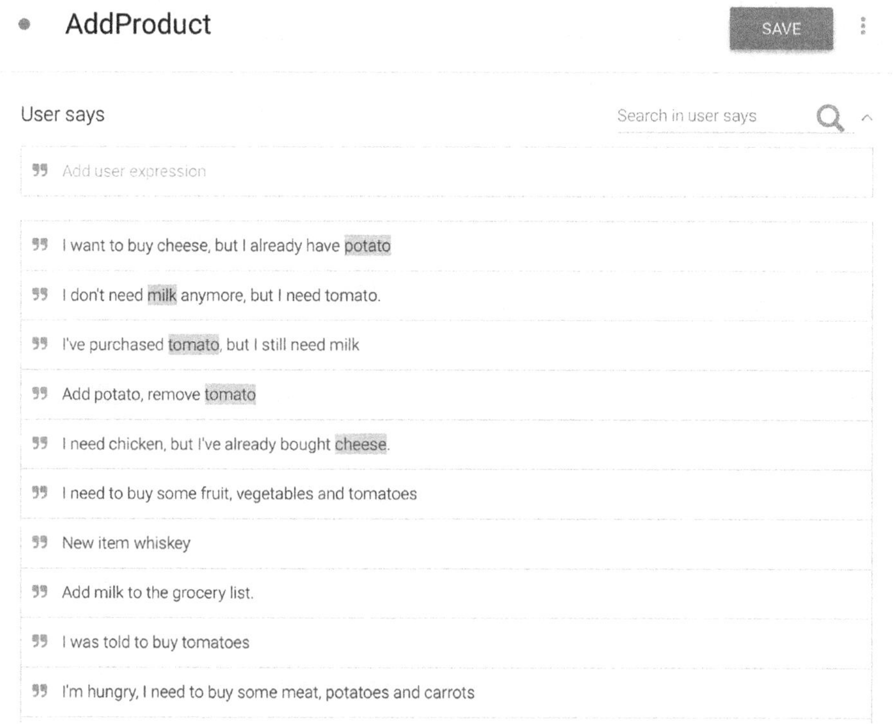

● AddProduct   SAVE   ⋮

User says   Search in user says   🔍 ⌃

> 🗨 Add user expression

🗨 I want to buy cheese, but I already have potato

🗨 I don't need milk anymore, but I need tomato.

🗨 I've purchased tomato, but I still need milk

🗨 Add potato, remove tomato

🗨 I need chicken, but I've already bought cheese.

🗨 I need to buy some fruit, vegetables and tomatoes

🗨 New item whiskey

🗨 Add milk to the grocery list.

🗨 I was told to buy tomatoes

🗨 I'm hungry, I need to buy some meat, potatoes and carrots

Figure 4-9. *Annotating entities in test sentences*

Note the types of sentences I've added. They are all different and look like real sentences that the user might say. The idea with these platforms is to enable free-flowing conversation with the users, not just a set of commands that the user must say, and the machine will try to match that with some strictly defined format. Users are not machines, and they can easily forget to say part of some command or maybe modify words and the order of the sentence. An intelligent system should be able to handle that, which is exactly what Dialogflow offers. The more examples you add, the more precise the response you will get.

Let's test this with a new sentence and see what response you get. There is a testing area in the Dialogflow dashboard on the right. The example is "Hmm...I think I want something to eat, maybe some meat." There's nothing similar in the provided samples. Figure 4-10 shows the response.

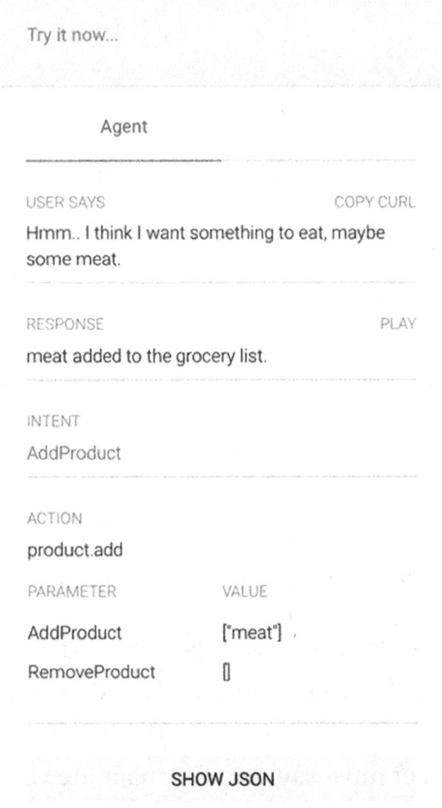

Try it now...

Agent

USER SAYS   COPY CURL
Hmm.. I think I want something to eat, maybe
some meat.

RESPONSE   PLAY
meat added to the grocery list.

INTENT
AddProduct

ACTION
product.add

PARAMETER   VALUE

AddProduct   ['meat']

RemoveProduct   []

SHOW JSON

Figure 4-10. *Testing the Dialogflow agent*

It correctly put "meat" in the group of added products, which is pretty awesome. You can try this with a few more new examples. If some of them are wrong, you can manually label the parameters in the sentence, retrain the model (that's a fancy way of saying click Save), and try again. Then you will see that the text is correctly handled. You need to follow the same steps for setting up the `RemoveProduct` intent, just with different examples and annotations.

You can also define context, which, as its name implies, can be used to get an idea of the previous state of the conversation with the user, before doing the request. This can be useful if you handle several requests in a row and you need to keep track of what was spoken before. For example, if the user says "Play me a U2 song" and after that "Play another one," then using contexts, Dialogflow can infer that the next song should also be from U2.

Another cool feature of api.ai is webhooks (in the "Fulfillment" section in Dialogflow). Webhook integration allows you to pass the extracted information from a phrase into a web service and get a result from it. For example, if your agent provides transport information with train departures, you can attach a webhook to a service that finds routes based on the location extracted from the Dialogflow service. You can solve the whole flow with only one request to the service. Otherwise, you would have to handle the response from Dialogflow and then send it to a routing service. If you have a web, iOS, and Android app, that's another additional implementation per platform. With webhooks, you don't need that.

If your app supports multiple languages, with the newer versions of the platform, this is now supported in the same agent. Previously, you had to create a separate new agent with a different access token. Based on the current language on the device, you would set the appropriate access token. But now, the platform enables you to add other languages, which means you need only one token. The platform does not support automatic translation. This means the agent with different language support has to be trained separately, with training sentences, intents, and entities specific for that language.

Integrating Dialogflow into the App

Now let's go back to your GroceryList app. How can you integrate everything discussed so far in your app? Api.ai provides native integrations for iOS and Android. You can, of course, directly connect to the REST API, but using the SDKs is the faster approach.

You can find the iOS SDK on GitHub. You will integrate it as a CocoaPod. Go ahead and create new Podfile with the contents shown in Listing 4-30. Note that the CocoaPod still has the old name, ApiAI.

Listing 4-30. Contents of the Podfile

```
use_frameworks!

target :SpeechPlayground do
   pod 'ApiAI'
end
```

Note CocoaPods is probably the most popular dependency management tool for iOS, along with Carthage. You can install it by typing the following command in your terminal: `sudo gem install cocoapods`. CocoaPods automatically creates and updates the Xcode workspace for your application and all its dependencies.

To install the dependencies, run `pod install` from the terminal, at the root of your project (where the Podfile is created). Open the generated `.xcworkspace` file, and the SDK should be there. All of the downloaded CocoaPods are located in the Pods folder, relative to the location of the Podfile.

You will create a wrapper of the ApiAI SDK in a new class called `ApiAIService`. This class will do the communication with the ApiAI SDK and return an `ApiAIResponse` struct (Listing 4-31), which will contain two arrays representing the added and removed products.

Listing 4-31. Struct Representing the api.ai Response

```
public struct ApiAIResponse {
    let addedProducts: [String]
    let removedProducts: [String]
}
```

In the `ApiAIService`, you are creating an instance of the `ApiAI` class, which will do the communication with the REST service of the platform. You need to provide `clientAccessToken` to the SDK, so please replace the placeholder value in that constant with your access token. You can get the client access token on the Settings screen for your agent in the Dialogflow dashboard (Figure 4-11).

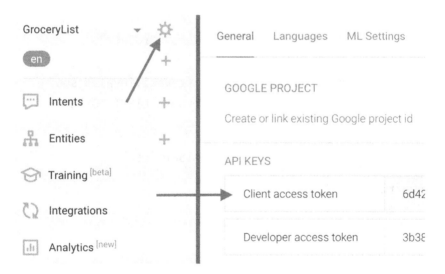

Figure 4-11. *Getting the client access token*

You are also defining two closures (`SuccesfullApiAIResponseBlock` and `FailureApiAIResponseBlock`), which will be used as callbacks in the `extractProducts(fromText:success:failure)` method, which is the

133

most important method in this class. This method takes the text you've already recognized using the Speech framework from the previous section and sends it to Dialogflow for analysis (Listing 4-32).

Listing 4-32. ApiAIService Implementation

```
public typealias SuccesfullApiAIResponseBlock =
(ApiAIResponse?) -> Swift.Void
public typealias FailureApiAIResponseBlock = (Error?) ->
Swift.Void

class ApiAIService: NSObject {
    static let resultKey = "result"
    static let parametersKey = "parameters"
    static let addProductKey = "AddProduct"
    static let removeProductKey = "RemoveProduct"
    static let errorCode = 777
    static let errorDomain = "com.mitrevski.invalidjson"
    static let clientAccessToken = "YOUR_CLIENT_TOKEN"

    private var apiAI = ApiAI()
    static let sharedInstance = ApiAIService()

    override init() {
        super.init()
        setupApiAI()
    }

    func extractProducts(fromText text: String,
                        success: SuccesfullApiAIResponseBlock!,
                        failure: FailureApiAIResponseBlock!) {
        let request = self.apiAI.textRequest()
        request?.query = text
        request?.setCompletionBlockSuccess({ [unowned self]
```

```
        (request, response) in
        if let response = response as? Dictionary<String,
        Any> {
            success(self.extractProducts(fromResponse:
            response))
        } else {
            let error = NSError(domain:ApiAIService.
            errorDomain,
                                code:ApiAIService.
                                errorCode,
                                userInfo:nil)
            failure(error)
        }
    }, failure: { (request, error) in
        failure(error)
    })
    self.apiAI.enqueue(request)
}

private func setupApiAI() {
    let configuration = AIDefaultConfiguration()
    configuration.clientAccessToken = ApiAIService.
    clientAccessToken
    self.apiAI.configuration = configuration
}
}
```

If the request is successful, you take the needed values from the JSON response and create an ApiAIResponse, which you are sending back in the success handler. In any other case, you are just returning an error.

Now let's see part of the JSON response you get from Dialogflow (Listing 4-33) when you say something like "I want to buy cheese, but I already have potato."

Listing 4-33. JSON Response from Dialogflow

```
{
  "lang": "en",
  "result": {
    "resolvedQuery": "I want to buy cheese, but I already have
    potato",
    "action": "product.add",
     "parameters": {
      "AddProduct": [ "cheese" ],
      "RemoveProduct": [ "potato" ]
    },
    "contexts": [],
    "score": 1
  },
  "sessionId": "6f56c3be-6f86-460e-815d-cc4de8f82a72"
  // other parts from the JSON which are not relevant for your
  app are excluded
}
```

There is a lot of interesting information here. For example, you can see how accurate the resolution of the query with the score property is. You can see information about contexts, whether webhooks are used, and everything else discussed earlier. What you are really interested in is the parameters section; you want to know what's inside the AddProduct and RemoveProduct lists so you can put them in the ApiAIResponse struct. To do this, you will add a new method for extracting the products from the response (Listing 4-34). In this method, you are going through the response dictionary until you get to the parameters section.

Listing 4-34. Extracting the Products from the Response in
ApiAIService

```
private func extractProducts(
    fromResponse response: Dictionary<String, Any>) ->
    ApiAIResponse? {
    var toBeAdded = [String]()
    var toBeRemoved = [String]()
    guard let result = response[ApiAIService.resultKey]
                        as? Dictionary<String, Any>
    else {
        return nil
    }
    guard let parameters = result[ApiAIService.parametersKey]
                            as? Dictionary<String, Any>
    else {
        return nil
    }
    if let addProducts = parameters[ApiAIService.addProductKey]
                            as? Array<String> {
        toBeAdded = addProducts
    }
    if let removeProducts = parameters[ApiAIService.remove
                        ProductKey]
                            as? Array<String> {
        toBeRemoved = removeProducts
    }
    return ApiAIResponse(addedProducts: toBeAdded,
                    removedProducts: toBeRemoved)
}
```

Now that you are done with the service, let's go back to the grocery list's ViewController. Since you will now properly handle the transcribed text, it's time to get rid of some improvisations you did. Delete the SpeechHelper class and all its related arrays, such as removalWords, sessionProducts, and deletedProducts. The code will now be cleaner and more robust, with only one array that keeps the products displayed in the list (addedProducts). This will also simplify your startRecording method; you just need to restart the timer there (Listing 4-35).

Listing 4-35. Updated Implementation of startRecording in the ViewController

```
func startRecording() {
        guard let inputNode = audioEngine.inputNode else {
            showAudioError()
            return
        }
        recognitionTask = speechRecognizer.recognitionTask(
            with: recognitionRequest!,
            resultHandler:{ [unowned self] (result, error) in
            var recognized: String?
            if result != nil {
                recognized = result?.bestTranscription.
                formattedString
                self.timer?.invalidate()
                self.timer = nil
                if !self.cancelCalled {
                    self.timer = Timer.scheduledTimer(withTime
                    Interval: 2,
```

```
                                            repeats:
                                            false,
                                      block: { _ in
                                   _ = self.handleStop()
                      })
         }
         self.recognizedText.text = recognized
      }
      var finishedRecording = false
      if result != nil {
          finishedRecording = result!.isFinal
      }
      if error != nil || finishedRecording {
          inputNode.removeTap(onBus: 0)
          self.handleFinishedRecording()
      }
   })
   let recordingFormat = inputNode.outputFormat(forBus: 0)
   inputNode.installTap(onBus: 0,
                        bufferSize: 1024,
                        format: recordingFormat) {
      [unowned self] (buffer, when) in
      self.recognitionRequest?.append(buffer)
   }
   startAudioEngine()
}
```

With your new implementation, you are extracting the products whenever you are finished with the recording. Apart from being cleaner, this is also faster than always iterating through the segments of the recognized text on the go. Let's take a look at the extractProducts(fromText:) method (Listing 4-36).

Listing 4-36. Extracting Products from Text in the ViewController

```
func extractProducts(fromText text: String) {
    ApiAIService.sharedInstance.extractProducts(fromText: text,
                                                success: {
        [unowned self] response in
        if let response = response {
            let toBeAdded = response.addedProducts
            let toBeRemoved = response.removedProducts
            var tmp = self.addedProducts
            tmp.append(contentsOf: toBeAdded)
            self.addedProducts = [String]()
            for product in tmp {
                if !toBeRemoved.contains(product) {
                    self.addedProducts.append(product)
                }
            }
            OperationQueue.main.addOperation() {
                self.productsTableView.reloadData()
            }
        }
    }) { error in
        print(error ?? "An error occured")
    }
}
```

The method calls the `ApiAIService` to get the products that need to be added and removed. The merging logic is similar to what you've seen before.

That completes your GroceryList app. You can test it with more complex queries (Figure 4-12). Your voice commands can be more natural, just like you would have said them to a person. If the agent doesn't recognize an intent or properly extract its entities, you can go to the training section in the Dialogflow dashboard and find the unresolved queries. If they make sense, then you can mark them and retrain the model, improving the quality of the agent. This good thing is that the training can continue after you ship the application to the App Store, without requiring an app update. That will also provide you with more data and example phrases.

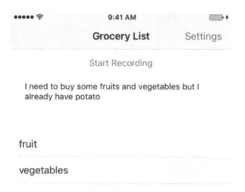

Figure 4-12. *Adding and removing items with more complex sentences*

Summary

Let's sum up what you did in this chapter. First, you started with the most basic approach of extracting the products from a spoken phrase—by matching hard-coded products. The goal of this project was to get to know the Speech framework, learn how to do recordings, and perform speech-to-text conversion. You familiarized yourself with audio engines, speech recognizers, recognition tasks, and more.

Next, you did the opposite—text-to-speech conversion, where the iPhone tells the user which products need to be purchased. Here, you used the AVSpeechSynthesizer class from AVFoundation.

141

Finally, in the third part of this chapter, you explored Dialogflow, a conversational interface platform. You replaced your simple matching words implementation with a trained agent from Dialogflow, and as a result, you were able to do much more complex queries for adding items or removing items to the list.

Figure 4-13 summarizes the complete implementation.

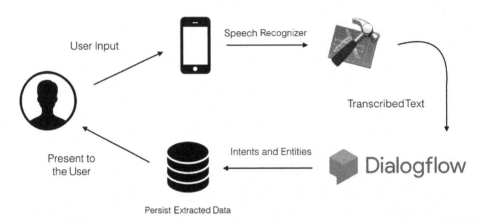

Figure 4-13. *Overview of the grocery list implementation*

After the spoken phrase is provided by the user, it is translated to plain text using the Speech framework. Then, the text is sent to Dialogflow, which processes the text and extracts the intent and the entities associated with it, returning a JSON response. You save this information and present it to the user in your table view.

CHAPTER 5

Getting Started with Wit.ai

As mentioned at the beginning of the book, all the big players are entering the exciting field of conversational interfaces. This means that Google's Dialogflow is not the only option for analyzing and understanding the user's spoken (or written) input. Facebook has its own product, called Wit.ai. In this chapter, you will explore Wit.ai and compare it to Dialogflow. Wit.ai's vision is to offer developers an open and extensible natural language platform that learns human language from every interaction. What's interesting is that everything that's learned is shared with all developers, which is quite useful because the platform is used by more than 120,000 developers.

The platform supports creating bots that can chat with humans on any messaging platform (for example, Facebook's Messenger). It provides integration with mobile apps, enabling voice interface to the apps, which is the most interesting feature for this book. It also supports home automation, meaning that you can, for example, set the temperature of the thermostat in your home using the platform. Interacting with wearable devices such as watches and with robots is another interesting feature of the platform.

© Martin Mitrevski 2018
M. Mitrevski, *Developing Conversational Interfaces for iOS*,
https://doi.org/10.1007/978-1-4842-3396-2_5

Creating a Grocery List App

To compare the platform with Dialogflow, you will build the same grocery list app that you developed in Chapter 4. To get started, you need to create an account on Wit.ai. You can do this by logging in with either Facebook or GitHub. After you do this, a default first app is created for you. Let's create a new app by clicking the plus icon in the toolbar at the top-right corner and call it GroceryList (Figure 5-1).

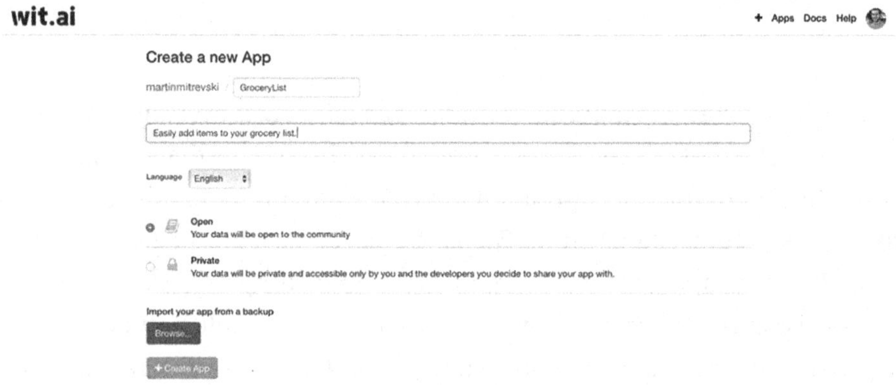

Figure 5-1. *Creating an app on the Wit.ai dashboard*

Just like Dialogflow, you first need to train the Wit.ai engine to start understanding the inputs. Here you don't need to define an intent. If you don't define it, a default one is used, as you will see later in the JSON response. When you create the application, a default entity called an *intent* is created. Click it and enter **product** as its name. You can assign roles to the entity. You need the service to be able to detect which products should be added to the grocery list and which ones should be removed. That's why you will define two roles: add and remove.

Creating roles on the Wit web site is not the most user-friendly experience. First, you need to type a sentence in the training dashboard on the home page of your application. Let's type **I want to buy milk**. Select the word *milk* since that will be your entity and click the plus icon to add a new entity. This will list the entities you support in the application, which in your case is the product entity. Select the product entity, which in turn will display a radio button with the ability to set a role (Figure 5-2). Set the role name to add. The next time you want to set a role to be product:add, you can just select it from the list of available entities. Click Validate to train the model with this new input.

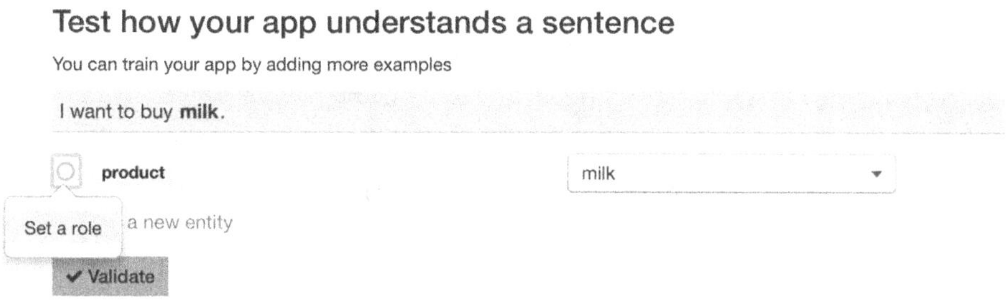

Test how your app understands a sentence

You can train your app by adding more examples

I want to buy **milk**.

product   milk

Set a role a new entity

✔ Validate

Figure 5-2. *Setting an add role for the entity*

Follow the same process to create a product:remove entity; in other words, type a sentence, mark the entity, and create a new role (Figure 5-3).

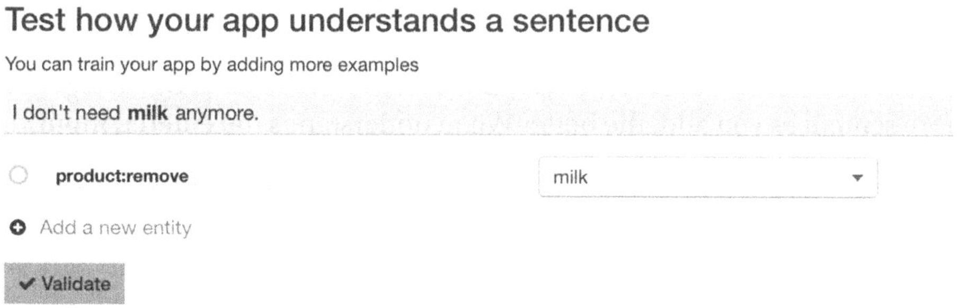

Test how your app understands a sentence

You can train your app by adding more examples

I don't need **milk** anymore.

product:remove   milk

➕ Add a new entity

✔ Validate

Figure 5-3. *Setting a remove role for the entity*

As you type sentences in the text field for training, you select the entities and define their roles (add or remove). You can also connect the entity to an existing value or create new one. For example, if you select *potatoes* and you already have *potato*, you should connect it to that value. Wit.ai will create a synonym for *potato* (Figure 5-4).

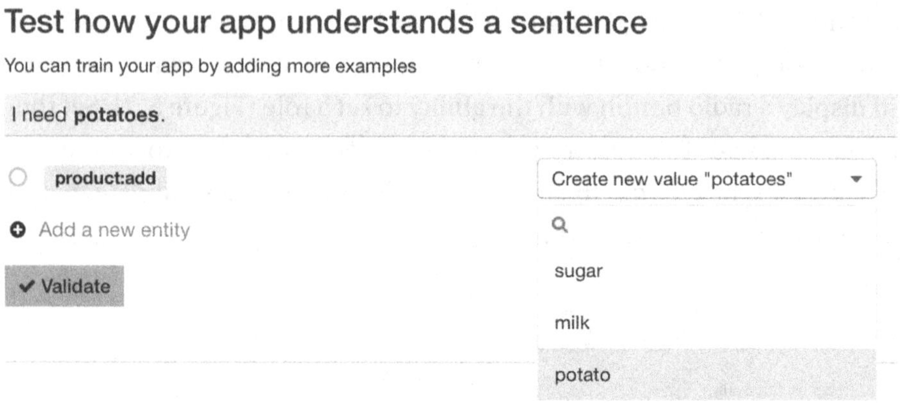

Test how your app understands a sentence

You can train your app by adding more examples

I need **potatoes**.

○ **product:add**	Create new value "potatoes" ▼
➕ Add a new entity	🔍
✔ Validate	sugar
	milk
	potato

Figure 5-4. *Defining a synonym for an entity value*

This enables users to say different forms of a word. In the end, the value will be resolved to the same entity. Adding new entity values and test sentences improves the intent detection and entities extraction in your app, without requiring an application update. To add more entity values (products), click the product entity on the home page. This will open the entity page, where you can see information about the roles it supports, as well as the keywords and expressions that are used in the training of the agent. In the Keywords section, type more products and define a few synonyms to improve the natural language understanding (Figure 5-5). The more sentences you add, the better Wit.ai understands the entered input.

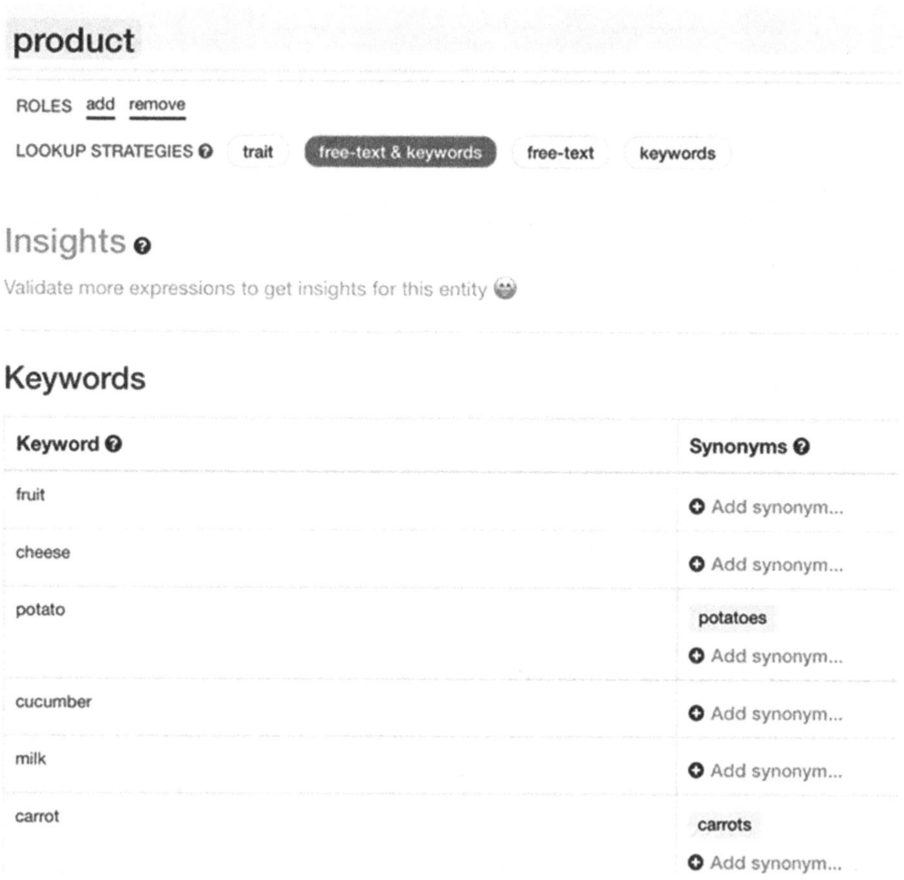

product

ROLES add remove

LOOKUP STRATEGIES ❓ (trait) (free-text & keywords) (free-text) (keywords)

Insights ❓

Validate more expressions to get insights for this entity 😶

Keywords

Keyword ❓	Synonyms ❓
fruit	➕ Add synonym...
cheese	➕ Add synonym...
potato	**potatoes** ➕ Add synonym...
cucumber	➕ Add synonym...
milk	➕ Add synonym...
carrot	**carrots** ➕ Add synonym...

Figure 5-5. *Synonyms for entities*

Below the keywords, you can see the sentences you have used to train the model. If you select a sentence, you can see what you have marked as an entity and the role assigned to it. This is handy if you have unpredictable results and you are not sure where are they coming from (Figure 5-6).

I'm hungry, I need to buy some **meat, potatoes** and **carrots**, but I don't need **cheese** anymore.

○ product:add	meat	▼
○ product:remove	cheese	▼
○ product:add	potato	▼
○ product:add	carrot	▼

➕ Add a new entity

[✔ Validate]   [✕ Cancel]

66 I'm hungry, I need to buy some meat, potatoes and carrots	✕
66 I want to buy whiskey	✕
66 I was told milk is not needed anymore.	✕
66 I have been told to buy fruit.	✕
66 I was told to buy some tomatoes.	✕
66 I don't need vegetables anymore.	✕
66 Remove vegetables	✕
66 Remove milk	✕
66 Add milk	✕

Figure 5-6. *Training sentences*

Another thing worth mentioning about Wit.ai is the Stories UI. This endpoint will be shut down soon, so I will not spend much time on it. I will just mention that developers were able to create replies that the bot would give for certain inputs, by creating stories. For example, for your case, after you say something like "I need milk," the bot might reply with "Milk added to your grocery list." It's being shut down mostly because the top apps that use Stories are using only one-turn replies (just like in your case). That's why Wit.ai is focusing on the Message endpoint since one-turn replies can be achieved with that endpoint as well.

Performing the iOS Implementation

Now, let's see how you can integrate Wit.ai in your iOS application. Create a new single-view application called WitAi or open the starter project provided with this chapter. Currently, Wit.ai has an iOS SDK, which is only community supported. The preferred way for nonexperimental apps is to use the HTTP API. However, the easiest way to integrate Wit.ai into your iOS application is with the iOS SDK. The SDK is available as a pod, so let's create a new Podfile with the contents from Listing 5-1. You can find more details about CocoaPods in Chapter 4. Make sure to review it if you are not sure how it works.

Listing 5-1. Podfile for Wit.ai

```
platform :ios, '10.0'
use_frameworks!

target :WitAi do
  pod 'Wit', '~> 4.2.1'
end
```

After running pod install from your terminal, which will install the dependency, open the generated workspace. To identify your application to Wit.ai, you need to provide the client access token to the SDK. The best place to set the token is on app start, in the applicationDidFinishLaunchingWithOptions method (Listing 5-2). You can find the token in the Settings section in the top-right corner of your Wit dashboard (Figure 5-7). Be careful with this section; the refresh icon on the right of the token regenerates it. If you have an app that is currently live, you will need to submit an update because with the previous token, the app would not be able to access the Wit.ai services. You can also implement a solution where the token is loaded from your server on app start. This will give you an option to update the token, without requiring an App Store update.

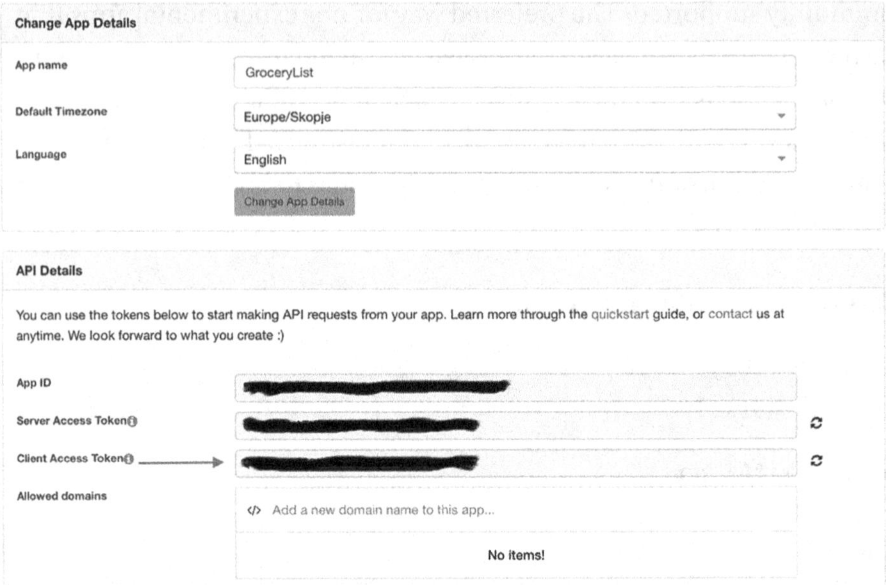

Figure 5-7. *Getting the Wit client access token*

Listing 5-2. Setting the Client Access Token

```
func application(_ application: UIApplication,
                 didFinishLaunchingWithOptions
                 launchOptions:
                         [UIApplicationLaunchOptionsKey:
                         Any]?)
-> Bool {
    Wit.sharedInstance().accessToken = "YOUR_CLIENT_ACCESS_TOKEN"
    return true
}
```

The user interface for this app will be the same as in the previous app. You will have one button for starting and stopping the recording, a text view to show the transcribed text, and a table view that will present the products in the grocery list. The UI is already set up in the starter project.

If you are building the project from scratch, make sure you have set up the required permissions about speech recognition and the microphone in your app's property list file (Figure 5-8).

▼ Information Property List		Dictionary	(16 items)
Privacy - Speech Recognition Usage Description	◇	String	Speech recognition needed for adding/removing items to the grocery list.
Privacy - Microphone Usage Description	◇	String	Microphone needed for recording your voice when you want to add/remove

Figure 5-8. *Permissions for speech recognition*

On iOS 10 and newer, the Wit SDK uses Apple's Speech framework. This means that a lot of the tasks you performed in the Dialogflow version of this app, by creating speech recognition request, speech recognition task, audio engine, and speech recognizer, are not needed here anymore since they are already implemented in the SDK. As you will see, there will be less code here.

Next, you need to set up Wit. The Wit SDK is accessible via a singleton shared instance.

Note   Singleton is a software design pattern that restricts the instantiation of a class to one object.

The `ViewController` that shows the list of items will implement the `WitDelegate` methods. You will see later which methods those are and how to implement them. You need to set the voice activity detection algorithm. There are three options here: `disabled` (which means no voice detection; you are in charge of everything), `detecting speech stop` (as the name implies, it detects only when the user stops talking), and `full` (which detects both the start and the stop of the user's speech). You will set the full speech stop detection. Next, you have `voice activity detection timeout`, which is the maximum length of time without speaking until the framework detects the stop of the speech. If you set it to -1, it will not have a timeout. The default value is 7,000 milliseconds (7 seconds). You will set this to 3,000 milliseconds.

After the timeout, you set the sensitivity setting of the voice detection algorithm. These values range from 0 to 100. The lower values are for strong voice signals, such as a cell phone or personal microphone. The higher values are for fixed-position microphones or any application with voice buried in ambient noise. The higher end looks more suitable to your use case, so you are going to set it to a max value of 100. Apart from these properties, you can set the speechRecognitionLocale setting, which is the locale used for speech recognition. The default is en_US, so you will not set anything there. Listing 5-3 shows the setup of these values. Call the method setupWit in the viewDidLoad method of the ViewController.

Listing 5-3. Setting Up the Wit Parameters

```
private func setupWit() {
    Wit.sharedInstance().delegate = self
    Wit.sharedInstance().detectSpeechStop = .full
    Wit.sharedInstance().vadTimeout = 3000
    Wit.sharedInstance().vadSensitivity = 100
}
```

You can provide a WitSession to the SDK, which will use the Converse endpoint (Stories UI), but since that API will be deprecated soon, you will stick to the Message endpoint, which is the default one. Also, if you open WitDelegate's methods, most of the methods such as didReceiveMergeEntities, didReceiveAction, and didReceiveMessage are from the Converse endpoint and will be removed soon. What you need is a method that will recognize every word as the user speaks and then detects whether the word is final. The witDidRecognizePreviewText delegate method provides that. The SDK passes the previewText flag (which is what is recognized until that point) and the isFinal flag (which indicates whether that is the final text the user has spoken).

In practice, the isFinal flag doesn't work that good. There are situations where the witDidRecognizePreviewText is not called for more than a minute and the isFinal flag is false, although there is no speech input for that period. This also prevents the recording from being stopped. Probably this is a bug in the SDK since the voice detection timeout is not taken into consideration. To solve this, you will create a timer, which will be stopped on every call of the witDidRecognizePreviewText callback and started again. If the method is not called for three seconds, you will stop the recording explicitly (Listing 5-4).

Listing 5-4. Implementing the Method Called When Text Is Recognized by Wit in the ViewController

```
private var timer: Timer? // defined at the beginning of the
ViewController.
@IBOutlet weak var transcriptedText: UITextView! // same as
timer.

func witDidRecognizePreviewText(_ previewText: String!,
                                final isFinal: Bool) {
    self.transcriptedText.text = previewText
    stopTimer()
    self.timer = Timer.scheduledTimer(withTimeInterval: 3,
                                repeats: false,
                                block: { [unowned self]
                                _ in
                                    self.handleStop()
                                })
}
```

```
private func handleStop() {
    Wit.sharedInstance().stop()
    recordingButton.setTitle("Start recording", for: .normal)
    stopTimer()
}

private func stopTimer() {
        self.timer?.invalidate()
        self.timer = nil
}
```

After you call the stop method of the Wit SDK, the witDidGraspIntent method is called. The parameters of this method are an array of possible outcomes, the ID of the message, customData (which is optional and can be passed in the start(customData) method in the SDK), and the error object (if an error occurred). In the array of outcomes, you need the first outcome: the one with the highest confidence factor. The outcome object is a dictionary, whose contents are shown in Listing 5-5.

Listing 5-5. The Outcome Object

```
{
    "_text" = "I want to buy milk";
    confidence = "<null>";
    entities =     {
        add =           (
                            {
                    "_body" = milk;
                    "_end" = 18;
                    "_entity" = product;
                    "_role" = add;
                    "_start" = 14;
                    confidence = "0.94597507156525";
                    type = value;
```

```
            value = milk;
        }
    );
};
intent = "default_intent";
}
```

At the root of the dictionary, you have information about the recognized text, the confidence of the text (which might be null), the extracted entities, and the intent. Note that you haven't defined an intent, so a default one is used. The most interesting part is the `entities` dictionary. It contains several keys for the entities defined in the Wit.ai web application. As you may recall, you defined two roles, add and remove, for the product entity. If one of them or both are recognized in a sentence, they will appear as keys in the entities dictionary. In your example, "I want to buy milk," only the add role is detected, which is correct, based on your training sentences.

The values of the keys in the entities dictionary are arrays; they contain all the detected entities for a given role. The values in those arrays are dictionaries themselves. There you can find information about each kind of entity, its role, the confidence factor, the type, and the value. The value is what you are interested in since that's what you will present to the user. Let's see how you can implement the `witDidGraspIntent` method, shown in Listing 5-6.

Listing 5-6. Implementing the witDidGraspIntent Delegate Method

```
func witDidGraspIntent(_ outcomes: [Any]!,
                       messageId: String!,
                       customData: Any!,
                       error: Error!) {
    if outcomes != nil && outcomes.count > 0 {
        let outcome = outcomes[0] as! [String : Any]
```

```
    guard let entities = outcome["entities"] as? [String :
    Any] else {
            return
    }
    updateProducts(fromEntities: entities)
    OperationQueue.main.addOperation {
        self.tableView.reloadData()
    }
  }
}
```

After checking whether you have at least one outcome, you check whether there is an entities entry in that outcome. If there is, you are extracting the add and remove entities of it, using the updateProducts method, and then you are updating the table view. Note that the delegate method might not be called from the main thread, so you need to make sure you take the main queue before doing any user interface action (in your case, reloading the table view data). Let's examine the extractProducts (Listing 5-7) and updateProducts (Listing 5-8) methods.

Listing 5-7. Extracting the Products

```
private func extractProducts(fromEntities entities: [String :
Any],
                                  key: String) -> [String] {
    guard let toBeAdded = entities[key] as? Array<[String :
    Any]> else {
        return []
    }

    var products = [String]()
    for product in toBeAdded {
        if let value = product["value"] as? String {
            products.append(value)
```

```
        }
    }

    return products
}
```

Listing 5-8. Updating the Products

```
private var addedProducts: [String] = [String]() // defined at
the beginning

private func updateProducts(fromEntities entities: [String :
Any]) {
    let newProducts = self.extractProducts(fromEntities:
    entities,
                                           key: "add")
    let toBeRemovedProducts = self.extractProducts
    (fromEntities: entities,
                                           key: "remove")
    var tmp = addedProducts
    tmp.append(contentsOf: newProducts)
    addedProducts = []
    for product in tmp {
        if !toBeRemovedProducts.contains(product) {
            addedProducts.append(product)
        }
    }
}
```

The extractProducts method takes a list of entities (dictionaries) and a key (add or remove) and returns an array of values of the given role entities (for example, milk). Then in the updateProducts method, those two arrays are merged with the already entered products (in previous

speech inputs). You create a new array, where you add all the newly
and previously added products. You then iterate over that array and
copy to the addedProducts array only those products that are not in the
toBeRemovedProducts array. The table view is populated with the data
from the addedProducts array (Listing 5-9).

Listing 5-9. Implementing the Table View Data Source Methods

```swift
func tableView(_ tableView: UITableView,
            numberOfRowsInSection section: Int) -> Int {
    return addedProducts.count
}

func tableView(_ tableView: UITableView,
            cellForRowAt indexPath: IndexPath) ->
            UITableViewCell {
    var cell: UITableViewCell? =
        tableView.dequeueReusableCell(withIdentifier:
        "ProductCell")
    if cell == nil {
        cell = UITableViewCell(style: .default,
                            reuseIdentifier: "ProductCell")
    }
    cell?.textLabel?.text = addedProducts[indexPath.row]
    return cell!
}
```

The last thing you need to do is to define what happens when the
recording button is tapped. Here you have two possible states; either
the recorder is running or it is not. When it's recording and the button is
tapped, you stop the recording. If it's not recording, then you start it using
Wit's start method (Listing 5-10).

Listing 5-10. Implementing the @IBAction of the Recording Button

```
@IBAction func recordingButtonClicked(sender: UIButton) {
        if Wit.sharedInstance().isRecording() {
            handleStop()
        } else {
            handleStart()
        }
}

private func handleStart() {
        Wit.sharedInstance().start()
        transcriptedText.text = ""
        recordingButton.setTitle("Stop recording", for:
        .normal)
}
```

If you run the app, start the recording, and give a voice command, you should get something similar to what you did in Chapter 3, with Dialogflow (Figure 5-9). With the example, you can see that the plural form of *potatoes* is resolved in *potato*, just like you defined it in the creation of the entities.

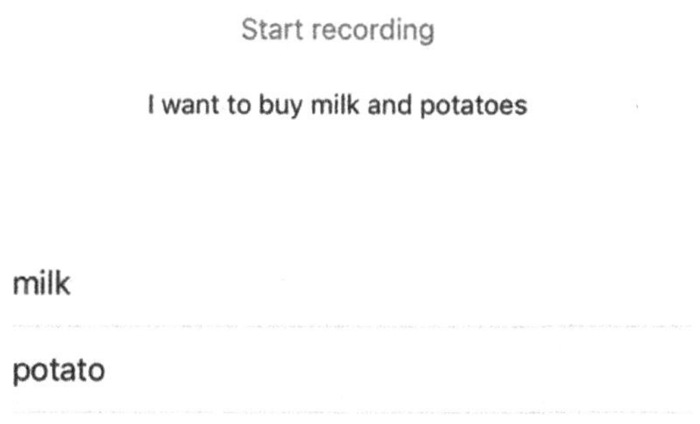

Start recording

I want to buy milk and potatoes

milk

potato

Figure 5-9. *Testing the Wit.ai implementation*

Using Wit.ai and Modern Objective-C Syntax

If you analyze the signature of `witDidGraspIntent` and the `witDidRecognizePreviewText` methods, you will see that the SDK is not optimized for Swift. The Wit iOS SDK is an Objective-C framework, but it doesn't have the modern Objective-C syntax.

Implementing Nullability Specifiers

First, it misses nullability specifiers (`nullable`, `nonnull`), and as a consequence, the parameters in the Wit functions are implicitly unwrapped. If the value in one of those functions is nil, the app will crash since you as a user of the Wit function expect the value to be non-nil (otherwise the type would be an optional type). To solve this, the SDK should specify the nullability specifiers in the Objective-C code. Those are annotations in the Objective-C code, which don't have any impact in an Objective-C project. When the framework is integrated in a Swift project, Swift will check the annotations and mark them as optional values if needed.

Implementing Lightweight Generics

Second, it doesn't use lightweight generics. In collections (arrays, sets, dictionaries) in Objective-C, you don't specify the type of the object. It can be anything. On the other hand, in Swift, when you declare an array, you have to specify the type of the elements. When collections in Objective-C don't have lightweight generic parameterization, they are translated in Swift as Any. You can see that in the outcomes array in the `witDidGraspIntent` method. This implies that the elements in the array can have any type, when in fact the array contains only dictionaries. The lightweight generics, like the nullability annotations, don't have any impact in the Objective-C code; you just declare what elements the array contains. You can still put different types in those arrays in Objective-C (although you shouldn't). You will just get a warning for this.

Besides these issues, the Wit.ai platform is pretty good. It's easy to set up and easy to train the models, and the results are pretty accurate.

Wit.ai vs. Dialogflow vs. Others

Comparing Wit.ai to Dialogflow, you have probably noticed that they have a few things in common. They were both acquired by big tech companies (Google and Facebook, respectively), and they are completely free. They use pretty good machine learning algorithms to provide accurate natural language understanding, even on new phrases. They have graphical user interfaces that let developers train the models with new sentences. However, Wit.ai's user interface is not that user friendly and intuitive. Both of them are based on the concept of intents and entities. There is support for predefined entities for date, color, temperature, and similar. You can attach webhooks on the services.

One thing that is better with Dialogflow is the integration with other APIs. At the moment, Wit.ai doesn't have quick and easy integration with Facebook Messenger or other messaging platforms. On the other hand, Dialogflow has one-click integrations, which let you connect the service to Google Assistant, Facebook Messenger, Slack, Viber, Twitter, Skype, and many other popular services.

Dialogflow has support for prebuilt agents that specialize in different areas of knowledge. You can use them directly, without additional training for the given domain. You can also customize the agents if needed.

The Small Talk module from Dialogflow is also a really cool feature that is currently not available on Wit.ai. This module allows you to easily import a lot of predefined answers to some common phrases and questions, in different contexts, such as courtesy, emotions, about the agent, hellos or goodbyes, and many others. What is great about the feature is that you can create your own Small Talk agent by providing different answers to the questions provided in those contexts. For example, you can create a nice chatbot, an arrogant one, or something else based on the answers provided. It's a really powerful feature that offers a lot of new possibilities for developers.

Using a Language-Understanding Intelligent Service

In addition to these two, there are also some other solutions on the market. For example, Microsoft has Language Understanding Intelligent Service (LUIS). You can make up to 10,000 requests to the service per month for free; after that, there are pricing models available. The service is available through REST endpoints, similarly to Dialogflow and Wit.ai. It is based on utterances, which are the textual input from the user that needs to be interpreted from the application. That input is then broken into tokens, and using machine learning algorithms, the intents and entities are extracted.

Let's see an example of how LUIS works. If the user says something like "Remind me to call my dad tomorrow," the JSON response from LUIS will have the contents displayed in Listing 5-11.

Listing 5-11. LUIS JSON Response

```
{
    "query": "remind me to call my dad tomorrow",
    "topScoringIntent": {
        "intent": "Reminder",
        "score": 0.9337804
    },
    "intents": [
        {
            "intent": "Reminder",
            "score": 0.9337804
        },
        {
```

```
        "intent": "None",
        "score": 0.0900467858
    }
],
    "entities": [
        {
            "entity": "tomorrow",
            "type": "builtin.datetime.date",
            "startIndex": 25,
            "endIndex": 32,
            "resolution": {
                "date": "2017-10-15"
            }
        }
    ]
}
```

From the JSON file, you can see that LUIS performs intent detection, returning the most likely intent in the topScoringIntent object, based on the score value. In addition, you can see the other intents that have lower scores, as well as a list of extracted entities. In the example, you can see that LUIS has prebuilt system entities, in this case for date. The entity tomorrow has a resolution entry, which is resolved based on the current date.

Using Amazon Lex

Amazon provides Alexa Skill Set and Amazon Lex. With Amazon Lex, the same natural understanding platform that is used by Amazon Alexa is available to developers. It can be integrated into mobile applications using the AWS Mobile SDK, as well as in Facebook Messenger, Slack, and Twilio. Amazon Lex has built-in integration with other Amazon services, such as AWS Lambda. The iOS SDK supports both voice and text as input and output. It can also detect when the user finishes speaking.

Using Watson IBM

IBM has Watson, which is more expensive and targeted to enterprises. It allows quick development and deployment of chatbots and virtual agents across a variety of channels, including mobile devices, messaging platforms, and robots. Virtual agents can be trained with domain knowledge specific to your business needs to provide automated services to the customers. It also has deep analytics, which provide insights on the customer's engagement with the agent. From the other services that IBM provides, there are speech-to-text and text-to-speech conversions, language translations, interpretations, and classifications, as well as predicting personality characteristics, needs, emotions, and social tendencies through written text.

There are many natural language–understanding platforms on the market. Things are changing pretty fast in this area, so you might expect a lot of improvements in this area in the future.

Summary

That wraps up the chapter. To sum up, you developed the same GroceryList application as in the previous chapter but using Facebook's Wit.ai. You saw how you can train the Wit.ai intents with test sentences and how to mark the found entities. Afterward, you integrated the Wit.ai iOS SDK into your GroceryList application. Since the speech detection part is already implemented in the SDK, you did not have to use the Speech framework directly. That reduced the code you had to write, compared to the Dialogflow implementation. You compared the two platforms, and you also saw other possibilities on the market.

CHAPTER 6

Natural Language Processing on iOS

Natural language processing (NLP) is a field in computer science that tries to analyze and understand the meaning of human language. It's quite a challenging topic, since computers find it pretty hard to understand what humans are trying to say (although they are perfect for executing commands well known to them). By utilizing established techniques, NLP analyzes the text, enabling applicability in the real world, such as automatic text summarization, sentiment analysis, topic extraction, named entity recognition, parts-of-speech tagging, relationship extraction, stemming, and more. NLP is commonly used for text mining, machine translation, and automated question answering.

NLP is also starting to get important in the mobile world. With the rise of conversational interfaces, extracting the correct meaning of the user's spoken input is crucial. For this reason, there are many NLP solutions on the two most popular platforms, iOS and Android. Since iOS 5, Apple has the `NSLinguisticTagger` class, which provides a lot of natural language processing functionalities in different languages. `NSLinguisticTagger` can be used to segment natural language text into paragraphs, sentences, or words, and tag information about those tokens, such as part of speech, lexical class, lemma, script, and language.

© Martin Mitrevski 2018
M. Mitrevski, *Developing Conversational Interfaces for iOS*,
https://doi.org/10.1007/978-1-4842-3396-2_6

Keyword Extraction

In this chapter, you will create a simple app that lists all the posts from my blog. When a post is selected, the app will open it in a web view, along with displaying details at the bottom of the screen about the detected language of the post and the most important words. You will accomplish this using the NSLinguisticTagger class and a simple implementation of the TF-IDF algorithm. There is a starter project accompanying this chapter, where the user interface and initial setup have already been prepared for you.

You will keep the posts in a local file called posts.json. Each entry stores information about the title and the URL of the post (Listing 6-1). The listing shows only part of the posts; you can find the full list in the starter project. Also, feel free to add your own posts, while keeping the same JSON structure.

Listing 6-1. JSON File with Post Information

```
{  "posts" : [
                {
                "title" : "Exploring Conversational Interfaces",
                "url" : "https://martinmitrevski.com/2017/02/25/
                exploring-conversational-interfaces/"
                },
                {
                "title" : "Algorithms in Swift",
                "url" : "https://martinmitrevski.com/2016/10/20/
                algorithms-in-swift/"
                },
                {
                "title" : "Swift Class Diagrams and more",
                "url" : "https://martinmitrevski.com/2016/10/12/
                swift-class-diagrams-and-more/"
```

```
        },
        {
        "title" : "Injecting code in iOS framework
        startup",
        "url" : "https://martinmitrevski.com/2016/08/27/
        injecting-code-in-ios-framework-startup/"
        }
    ]
}
```

The user interface of the app is pretty simple, consisting of a table view displaying the list of posts (Figure 6-1).

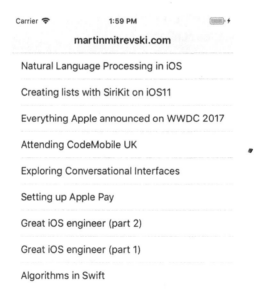

Figure 6-1. *User interface of the app*

First, you need to load the posts from the local JSON file into memory (Listing 6-2). Call the `loadPosts` method in the `viewDidLoad` method of the `ViewController`.

Listing 6-2. Loading the Posts from the Local JSON File

```swift
private var posts: [[String : String]]! // defined as var in
ViewController.

private func loadPosts() {
        let fileUrl = Bundle.main.url(forResource: "posts",
        withExtension: "json")
        do {
            let data = try Data(contentsOf: fileUrl!)
            let json = try JSONSerialization.jsonObject(with:
            data, options: .allowFragments)
                as! [String: Array<[String : String]>]
            posts = json["posts"]
            preloadSearchData()
        } catch {
            print("error loading posts")
        }
    }
```

After the posts are loaded, you preload the search data. This precomputation is done only once, at the start of the app. You save those results and reuse them whenever you need to compute the keywords for a given post (Listing 6-3).

Listing 6-3. Preloading the Search Data in ViewController.swift

```swift
private func preloadSearchData() {
        for post in posts {
            let url = post["url"]!
            load(url: url)
        }
}
```

You will get the contents of each URL, strip the HTML tags (since you don't want them to be included in the importance of the words), and count occurrences of a given word in each of the documents. You will use this information later with the TF-IDF algorithm for extracting the keywords. Don't worry—I will explain the TF-IDF algorithm later in the chapter.

In the `load(url:)` method, shown in Listing 6-4, you first create a request with the URL of the post (Listing 6-5) and then use an object of the `NSURLSession` that is executing the request. The word processing is done in the callback of the data task. You first remove the HTML tags (Listing 6-6). This is accomplished using the `String` class method for replacing occurrences of a string with a regular expression. Since `removeTags` is a utility method, create a new Swift file called `Utils.swift` and add the function there. Afterward, you extract the words with the `words(inText:url:action)` method, which you will examine in Listing 6-8.

Now, let's see which action you should provide to the `words(inText:url:action)` method. As mentioned, you need to count how many times each word appears in any of the documents. For this, you will use a variable called `wordCountings`. This will be a dictionary, where the key is the word, and the value is another dictionary, whose keys are the URL of the blog post, and the value is the count (how many times the word appears in that URL). Listing 6-7 shows this structure.

For the TF-IDF algorithm, you also need to know how many words every post has. You don't want to over-complicate `wordCountings`, so you will define another dictionary, `documentSizes`, which will have the URL of the post as a key and the total number of words in the document as a value.

Listing 6-4. Filling with Data the wordCountings and documentSizes Dictionaries in ViewController.swift

```
private var wordCountings = Dictionary<String,
Dictionary<String, Int>>()
```

```swift
private func load(url urlString: String){
  let task = session.dataTask(with:self.request(fromUrlString:
  urlString))
      { [unowned self] (data, response, error) in
      let html = String(data: data!, encoding: String.
      Encoding.utf8)
      var docSize = 0
      self.words(inText: removeTags(fromHtml: html!),
                url: urlString,
                action: {
          [unowned self] tag, tokenRange, stop, url in
          if let lemma = tag?.rawValue {
              docSize += 1
              if self.wordCountings[lemma] == nil {
                  self.wordCountings[lemma] =
                  Dictionary<String, Int>()
              }
              if self.wordCountings[lemma]![url] == nil {
                  self.wordCountings[lemma]![url] = 0
              }
              self.wordCountings[lemma]![url] =
                    self.wordCountings[lemma]![url]! + 1
          }
      })
      self.documentSizes[urlString] = docSize
  }
  task.resume()
}
```

Listing 6-5. Creating the Request for the Data Task in ViewController.swift

```swift
private func request(fromUrlString urlString: String) ->
URLRequest {
        let url = URL(string: urlString)
        let request = URLRequest(url: url!)
        return request
}
```

Listing 6-6. Removing the HTML Tags from a String in Utils.swift

```swift
func removeTags(fromHtml html: String) -> String {
    return html.replacingOccurrences(of: "<[^>]+>",
                                     with: "",
                                     options: String.Compare
                                     Options.regularExpression,
                                     range: nil)
}
```

Listing 6-7. Word Counting Structure

```
{
        "ios" : {
                "url1" : 1,
                "url2" : 5
        },
        "siri" : {
                "url1" : 2,
                "url2" : 0
        }
}
```

The method words(inText:url:action) receives some text and the corresponding URL as input; it finds the words using the linguistic tagger, and it invokes a completion handler (action) provided by the caller (Listing 6-8). You use this helper method both for counting the words and for computing the importance of the words.

Listing 6-8. Extracting the Words from Text in ViewController.swift

```
private func words(inText text: String,
                   url: String,
                   action: @escaping (NSLinguisticTag?,
                                      NSRange,
                                      UnsafeMutablePointer
                                      <ObjCBool>,
                                      String)
-> Void) {
    let tagger = NSLinguisticTagger(tagSchemes:[.lemma],
    options: 0)
    tagger.string = text
    let range = NSRange(location:0, length: text.utf16.count)
    let options: NSLinguisticTagger.Options =
            [.omitWhitespace, .omitPunctuation, .joinNames]

    tagger.enumerateTags(in: range,
                    unit: .word,
                    scheme: .lemma,
                    options: options) { tag, tokenRange,
                    stop in
                            action(tag, tokenRange, stop,
                            url)
                    }
}
```

Let's see what's happening here. You create an instance of the NSLinguisticTagger class, with lemma provided as a tag scheme.

Note   *Lemmatization* is the process of handling different forms of a word as a single item. For example, you want to treat the verb *do* in all its different forms (*doing*, *does*) as a one word since you are more interested in the importance of the word's semantics, not its syntax.

In addition to the lemma, there are lots of other tag schemes that the linguistic tagger supports. For example, you can use nameType, which classifies tokens that are part of named entities. There's also lexicalClass, which classifies tokens according to their class—part of speech for words, type of punctuation or whitespace, and so on. You can also tag tokens based on their most likely language. Check the NSLinguisticTagScheme struct for more details.

After the tagger is created, you set the provided text (which in this case is the stripped HTML text), and you define the range of the string. Then, you need to provide the options of the tagger. Here you set the omitWhitespace, omitPunctuation, and joinNames options. The first two are for ignoring the whitespace and the punctuation, as their names imply. The joinNames option is to handle people's names and surnames as one entry. For example, Tim Cook would be handled as one token.

When everything is set up, you call the enumerateTags(in:, unit:, scheme:, options:) method. This is a new method, starting with iOS 11, which will segment the string into tokens for the given unit and return those ranges along with a tag for any scheme in its array of tag schemes.

The new thing here is the unit parameter (word in this case, but you can also provide sentence, paragraph, or document). If you have to target an iOS version older than 11, there are enumerateTags methods that do not specify a unit act at the word level, starting with iOS 5.

Filling the data about the document sizes and word counts enables faster computation of the keywords for a given article. The computation will happen on a tap of a selected post. You will not store any computation or already loaded HTML (implementing a caching mechanism). That's why with a tap on a post, you will load the selected URL again, split the HTML into words, and then provide a different action (this time the TF-IDF algorithm) to the words method. The task called extractKeywordsTask does this (Listing 6-9).

Listing 6-9. The Extract Keywords Task

```
private func extractKeywordsTask(fromUrlString urlString:
String)
-> URLSessionDataTask {
    var result = [String : Double]()
    let task =
        session.dataTask(with: self.request(fromUrlString:
        urlString))
        { [unowned self] (data, response, error) in
            self.selectedHtml = String(data: data!,
                                       encoding: String.
                                       Encoding.utf8)
        self.words(inText: removeTags(fromHtml: self.
        selectedHtml!),
                    url: urlString,
                    action: {
                      [unowned self] tag, tokenRange, stop,
                      url in
                      if let lemma = tag?.rawValue {
                        result[lemma] = tfIdf(urlString:
                        urlString,
```

```
                                        word: lemma,
                                        wordCountings:
                                         self.word
                                         Countings,
                                        totalWordCount:
                                        self.document
                                        Sizes[url]!,
                                        totalDocs:
                                        self.posts.
                                        count)
                }
        })

        DispatchQueue.main.sync {
            self.keywords = Array(self.sort(result: result)
            [0..<10])
            self.loadingView.hide()
            self.performSegue(withIdentifier:
            "showWebView",
                            sender: self)
        }
    }
    return task
}
```

Here you create the request and start a session task. When the request finishes, you perform similar steps to the previous method for filling in the document sizes and word counts. The difference is that now, in the action block, you fill the result dictionary, which contains the TF-IDF value for each word.

TF-IDF Algorithm

I've mentioned this algorithm few times now, but I haven't explained it.

Note   *Term frequency–inverse document frequency* (TF-IDF) is a
numerical statistics method that is intended to reflect how important
a word is to a document in a collection of documents.

The first part, term frequency (TF), is about how many times a term occurs
in a document. You've already computed the occurrences of a word in a
document in your wordCountings dictionary. You just need to retrieve it
from there and divide it with the total word count in all documents. However,
if the word for some reason does not exist in the dictionary, the method will
return the Integer minimum value since you don't want that word to have
an impact in the computation of the TF-IDF value (Listing 6-10). Add this
function in the Utils.swift file created earlier.

Listing 6-10. Computing the Term Frequency in Utils.swift

```swift
func tf(urlString: String,
       word: String,
       wordCountings: Dictionary<String, Dictionary<String, Int>>,
       totalWordCount: Int)
    -> Double {
    guard let wordCounting = wordCountings[word] else {
        return Double(Int.min)
    }
    guard let occurrences = wordCounting[urlString] else {
        return Double(Int.min)
    }
    return Double(occurrences) / Double(totalWordCount)
}
```

Since there are words like *the*, which appear often but are not
important for the meaning of the text, the inverse document frequency

is introduced. With inverse document frequency (IDF), you count how many times a word appears in other documents. If it appears a lot (like *the* will), the weight of a word is diminished. You already have the countings value for a word in all documents in wordCountings, so you only need to ignore the number of occurrences of the current document and sum the other ones. The IDF factor will then be computed using a logarithm of the division of the total number of posts with the sum (Listing 6-11). Put this function in the Utils.swift file.

Listing 6-11. Inverse Document Frequency Computation

```swift
func idf(urlString: String,
        word: String,
        wordCountings: Dictionary<String, Dictionary<String,
        Int>>,
        totalDocs: Int)
    -> Double {
    guard let wordCounting = wordCountings[word] else {
        return 1
    }
    var sum = 0
    for (url, count) in wordCounting {
        if url != urlString {
            sum += count
        }
    }
    if sum == 0 {
        return 1
    }
    let factor = Double(totalDocs) / Double(sum)
    return log(factor)
}
```

After the TF and IDF are computed, they are multiplied to get the total TF-IDF weight (Listing 6-12). This is the reason you return 1 for the IDF factor when a word doesn't exist in the wordCountings dictionary.

Listing 6-12. Computing the TF-IDF Weight in Utils.swift

```
func tfIdf(urlString: String,
           word: String,
           wordCountings: Dictionary<String, Dictionary<String,
           Int>>,
           totalWordCount: Int,
           totalDocs: Int)
    -> Double {
    return tf(urlString: urlString,
             word: word,
             wordCountings: wordCountings,
             totalWordCount: totalWordCount)
        * idf(urlString: urlString,
             word: word, wordCountings: wordCountings,
             totalDocs: totalDocs)
}
```

After the word weights are computed, you sort them by those weights to get the top ten most important keywords for a post (Listing 6-13). Add this function in the ViewController.swift file.

Listing 6-13. Sorting the Results

```
private func sort(result: [String : Double]) -> [String] {
    let sorted = result.sorted(by: { (arg0, arg1) -> Bool in
        let (_, value1) = arg0
        let (_, value2) = arg1
```

```
            return value1 > value2
        }).map({ (arg) -> String in
            let (title, _) = arg
            return title
        })
        return sorted
}
```

Next, let's see the UITableView data source and delegate methods in ViewController. The data source is the posts array, which contains the data from the local JSON file posts.json (Listing 6-14).

Listing 6-14. UITableViewDataSource Methods

```
func tableView(_ tableView: UITableView,
                        numberOfRowsInSection section: Int)
                        -> Int {
        return posts.count
}

func tableView(_ tableView: UITableView,
                        cellForRowAt indexPath: IndexPath) ->
                        UITableViewCell {
        var cell = tableView.dequeueReusableCell(withIdentifi
        er: cellIdentifier)
        if cell == nil {
            cell = UITableViewCell(style: .default,
            reuseIdentifier: cellIdentifier)
        }
        let post = posts[indexPath.row]
        let title = post["title"]!
        cell?.textLabel?.text = title
        return cell!
}
```

When the user clicks a post, the tableView(_, didSelectRowAtIndexPath) is called, where you start the task for extracting the keywords (Listing 6-15) .

Listing 6-15. Table View Delegate Method Implementation

```
func tableView(_ tableView: UITableView,
                        didSelectRowAt indexPath: IndexPath) {
    tableView.deselectRow(at: indexPath, animated: true)
    selectedRow = indexPath
    let post = posts[indexPath.row]
    let urlString = post["url"]!
    loadingView.show()
    extractKeywordsTask(fromUrlString: urlString).resume()
}
```

The loadingView is already set up in the starter project in the ViewController. It is a user interface (.xib file), which is loaded in the viewDidLoad method by calling setupLoadingView (Listing 6-16). Make sure you use the LoadingView class provided in the starter project.

Listing 6-16. Setting Up the loadingView

```
private var loadingView: LoadingView! // defined as var in
ViewController

private func setupLoadingView() {

        loadingView = Bundle.main
            .loadNibNamed("LoadingView", owner: self, options:
            nil)?[0] as! LoadingView
        loadingView.frame = self.view.frame
        loadingView.isHidden = true
        self.view.addSubview(loadingView)

}
```

When the task finishes, the segue showWebView is performed, where you pass all the data (post title, keywords, HTML) that is needed by the WebViewController. The prepare(forSegue:sender) method is your chance to pass that data to the next controller (Listing 6-17).

Listing 6-17. Passing Data to the WebViewController

```
override func prepare(for segue: UIStoryboardSegue, sender:
Any?) {
        if segue.identifier == "showWebView" {
            let next = segue.destination as! WebViewController
            next.postTitle = posts[selectedRow!.row]["title"]
            next.html = selectedHtml
            next.keywords = keywords
            selectedRow = nil
            selectedHtml = nil
            keywords = nil
        }
}
```

Now, let's switch to the WebViewController, which will display the loaded HTML and the extracted keywords (see Listing 6-18). The HTML is loaded in a web view.

Listing 6-18. WebViewController Implementation

```
let languageTagger = NSLinguisticTagger(tagSchemes:
[.language], options: 0)

override func viewDidLoad() {
        super.viewDidLoad()
        self.title = postTitle
        tags.text = keywords.joined(separator: " ")
        webView.loadHTMLString(html, baseURL: nil)
```

```
        detectLanguage()
}

private func detectLanguage() {
        languageTagger.string = postTitle
        let language = languageTagger.dominantLanguage!
        detectedLanguage.text = "Detected language: \
        (language)"
}
```

If you run the app and select one post, you should have the keywords listed at the bottom of the screen (Figure 6-2). You can see that although the algorithm is pretty simple, the results are good. Of course, they are not perfect, but for that you would need more advanced algorithms.

You may have noticed one more detail above the keywords on the screenshot—the detected language. The detectLanguage method enables this information. It uses a new property introduced in iOS 11, called dominantLanguage of the linguistic tagger. By providing the language as a tagScheme when initializing the NSLinguisticTagger, you can provide a string, and the tagger tries to retrieve the language of that string. If it can't determine the language, the tagger returns the und value.

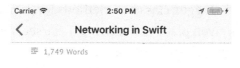

Carrier 🛜   2:50 PM   ⭤ 🔋⚡

‹   **Networking in Swift**

☰ 1,749 Words

Networking in Swift

Introduction

Connecting the mobile apps with a REST service is almost inevitable in every project – apps would be useless and boring if they don't get the latest data from the servers. There are a lot of great frameworks that do this for iOS, like AFNetworking and its Swift counterpart AlamoFire, Moya, APIKit and many more. They have their design differences, however at the core they are all wrappers of Apple's NSURLSession or NSURLConnection.

Detected language: en

promise creation HTTP chain synchronous execute wrapper rest core connection

Figure 6-2. *Extracted keywords for a blog post*

Showing Orthography

You can also check the orthography for a given string. *Orthography* is a description of the linguistic content of a text, usually used for spelling and grammar checking. Apple's `NSOrthography` class has methods to get the scripts that the text contains, the dominant language, the language map, and all the languages and scripts. Scripts are defined by four-letter tags and can have values such as `Latn`, `Grek`, `Cyrl`, and so on. Languages are described by BCP-47 tags, which is a standard for identifying languages. For example, for English, the tag would be en.

183

The NSLinguisticTagger class has methods for getting and setting the orthography at a given place of the string. Let's see how you can do this for the post title (Listing 6-19). Call the checkOrthography method in the viewDidLoad of the WebViewController, after the detectLanguage method.

Listing 6-19. Reading the Orthography of a String

```
private func checkOrthography() {
        languageTagger.string = postTitle
        var range = NSRange(location: 0, length: postTitle.count)
        if let ortoghraphy = languageTagger.orthography(at: 0,
        effectiveRange: &range) {
            print(ortoghraphy.dominantScript)
            print(ortoghraphy.dominantLanguage)
            print(ortoghraphy.languageMap)
            print(ortoghraphy.allLanguages)
        }
    }
```

As you can see in the method, you first create a range of the string, which in this case is the range of the post title. Then, you try to get the orthography of the string using the orthography(at:, effectiveRange:) method. If the orthography is not nil, you print the values of dominantScript, dominantLanguage, languageMap, and allLanguages. If you check the Xcode debug area, you will see the Latn value for the dominant script, the en dominant language, a dictionary with the script as the key and the language as the value, and an array of languages (only en in this case) for the allLanguages array.

Summary

With NLP methods, computers and mobile devices try to understand human language. `NSLinguisticTagger` from Apple's AVFoundation framework is a powerful class, with lots of possibilities for developers to make their apps smarter and more aware through NLP methods. In the chapter, you used it to extract keywords from blog posts. You first loaded the posts' HTML files and stripped any unnecessary data. Then you extracted the lemmatized words, using methods from `NSLinguisticTagger`. Afterward, you precomputed the occurrences of the words in every document. You used these calculations to compute the TF-IDF weight of those words. By doing that, you were able to get the keywords of every blog post. Also, you saw how to use `NSLinguisticTagger` to detect what the language is and the orthography of a given text.

CHAPTER 7

Sentiment Analysis with Core ML

What exactly is *machine learning*, a term that's pretty popular at the moment? Machine learning allows computers to learn and make decisions without being explicitly programmed on how to do something. This is accomplished by algorithms that iteratively learn from the data provided. It's a complex topic and an exciting field for researchers, data scientists, and academia. However, lately, it's starting to be a must-know skill for good tech people in general. Regular users expect apps to be smarter, to learn from their previous decisions, and to give recommendations for their future actions. For example, when you are listening to songs in YouTube-generated playlists, you expect the next song to be tailored to your musical taste. You expect Gmail to filter out and not bother you with all the spam e-mails. You expect Siri to know exactly what you mean with your spoken phrases. Machine learning is all the magic behind the scenes that makes all this work. Since conversational interfaces would not work without this magic, you will explore it on iOS in this chapter.

As a software engineer, you must be aware of the capabilities of machine learning and how it might improve your applications. Apple is also expecting you to catch up with these technologies by announcing Core ML, which enables the integration of already trained learning models into iOS apps. Developers can use trained models from popular deep learning frameworks, such as Caffe, Keras, scikit-learn, LIBSVM,

© Martin Mitrevski 2018
M. Mitrevski, *Developing Conversational Interfaces for iOS*,
https://doi.org/10.1007/978-1-4842-3396-2_7

and XGBoost. Using coremltools and Python scripts provided by Apple, you can convert trained models from the frameworks mentioned to the iOS Core ML model. This model can easily be integrated into an iOS application. The predictions happen on the device, using both the GPU and the CPU (depending on what's more appropriate at the moment). This means you don't need an Internet connection or to use an external web service (such as Dialogflow, for example) to provide intelligence to your apps. Also, the predictions are pretty fast. It's a powerful framework but with lots of restrictions, as you will see later.

Classifying Movie Reviews

In this chapter, you will build an app that will do text analysis in a different way than you have so far. It will classify movie reviews as positive and negative. Users will be able to add movies and provide reviews for them. The app will automatically group the reviews based on an already trained dataset (Figure 7-1). The subfield of artificial intelligence that does this is called *sentiment analysis*.

Note   Sentiment analysis is the process of computationally identifying and categorizing opinions expressed in a piece of text, especially to determine whether the writer's attitude toward a particular topic is positive, negative, or neutral.

In conversational interfaces, sentiment analysis is perfect for developing chatbots, which based on a user's sentiment can do different actions. In this case, if you have to respond to every movie review, you can predict the sentiment and return a random, predefined response (depending on whether the feedback is positive or negative).

Figure 7-1. *Using Core ML to determine whether a review is positive or negative*

Creating a Core ML Model

Finding an appropriate trained model to convert to the Core ML format can be tricky. Apple's coremltools is still in its early stages, which means it is still incomplete and can't support a lot of trained models. You will use a model trained with TF-IDF weighted word count extraction, described in the previous chapter. The training and testing are done with the scikit-learn framework. The resulting model is Linear Support Vector Machine (LinearSVM), which is trained with a TF-IDF vectorized dataset. Support vector machines are supervised learning models used for classification and regression analysis.

Note   If you are not comfortable with Python scripting, you can skip this part and go directly to the iOS app implementation. The Core ML model, which is the result of the following Python code, is already included in the starter project for this chapter; it's called MovieReviews.mlmodel. However, the following code might be useful if you decide to create your own models.

After you have created a model in the scikit-learn framework, you have to convert it to Core ML using coremltools. The resulting script, called convertToCoreML.py, loads the dataset, trains and tests the model in the scikit-learn framework, and converts it to a Core ML model, as shown in Listing 7-1. To run the scripts in this section, you will need Python version 2.7, coremltools (which can be installed with pip install -U coremltools), NumPy (which can be installed via brew install numpy), scikit-learn (which can be installed with pip install -U scikit-learn), and Tensorflow (the installation for Mac is available at https://www. tensorflow.org/install/install_mac/).

Listing 7-1. Creating a Core ML Model

```
import os
import numpy as np
from sklearn.metrics import confusion_matrix
from sklearn.svm import LinearSVC
from sklearn.feature_extraction.text import TfidfVectorizer
from coremltools.converters import sklearn
from sklearn.feature_extraction import DictVectorizer
from sklearn.model_selection import train_test_split

def make_Corpus(root_dir):
    polarity_dirs = [os.path.join(root_dir,f) for f in
    os.listdir(root_dir)]
    corpus = []

    for polarity_dir in polarity_dirs:
        sentiment = 'bad' if polarity_dir == 'txt_sentoken/neg'
        else 'good'
        reviews = [os.path.join(polarity_dir,f) for f in
        os.listdir(polarity_dir)]
        for review in reviews:
            reviewInfo = [sentiment]
```

```python
            doc_string = "";
            with open(review) as rev:
                for line in rev:
                    doc_string = doc_string + line
            reviewInfo.append(doc_string)
            if not corpus:
                corpus = [reviewInfo]
            else:
                corpus.append(reviewInfo)
    return corpus

root_dir = 'txt_sentoken'
corpus = make_Corpus(root_dir)
corpus = np.array(corpus)
X = corpus[:, 1]
y = corpus[:, 0]

X_train, X_test, y_train, y_test = train_test_split(X, y,
test_size=0.15, random_state=22)


vectorizer = TfidfVectorizer()
vectorized = vectorizer.fit_transform(X)
words = open('words_ordered.txt', 'w')
for feature in vectorizer.get_feature_names():
    words.write(feature.encode('utf-8') + '\n')
words.close()
model = LinearSVC()
model.fit(vectorized, y)
coreml_model = sklearn.convert(model)
coreml_model.save('MovieReviews.mlmodel')
```

Before you run the script, you need the movie reviews polarity dataset (available at https://www.cs.cornell.edu/people/pabo/movie-review-data/). After you have downloaded the dataset, you need to put it in the same directory where the script is located (the root of the project in this case), in a subdirectory called txt_sentoken. The txt_sentoken directory should contain two subdirectories, called neg and pos. In these directories, the positive and negative movie reviews are classified. To run the script, type python convertToCoreML.py in the terminal at the root of the project.

In the script, you go through both the positive and negative review directories, and you append the sentiment (which can be either bad or good) as the first element in an array and the actual review as a second. After you have collected the data in an array, you convert it to a multidimensional array using the popular Python extension package NumPy.

Note   You are using a multidimensional array since it's memory efficient and provides fast numerical operations.

You create a training and testing set with the function train_test_split, which splits arrays or matrices into random train and test subsets. Afterward, you create TfidfVectorizer, which converts a collection of raw documents to a matrix of TF-IDF features. You also create a new text file called words_ordered.txt with all the words of the vectorizer (you will need this later). This vectorized data is used to create the LinearSVC model, which is then converted to the Core ML format, using the scikit-learn converter from coremltools.

If you open this model in Xcode, you will see some basic information about it, the Swift-generated code that you can use in your app, and the input and output parameters (Figure 7-2).

The input format defines what the model expects to receive to provide prediction based on the training set. You might have expected a string (movie review) as an input to the model, which returns whether the sentiment is good or bad. However, here you have `MLMultiArray`, which is a multidimensional array used as input to most Core ML models (you can also send images to the models, but that's not applicable to this app). This array has a dimension of 39659. How do you create such input?

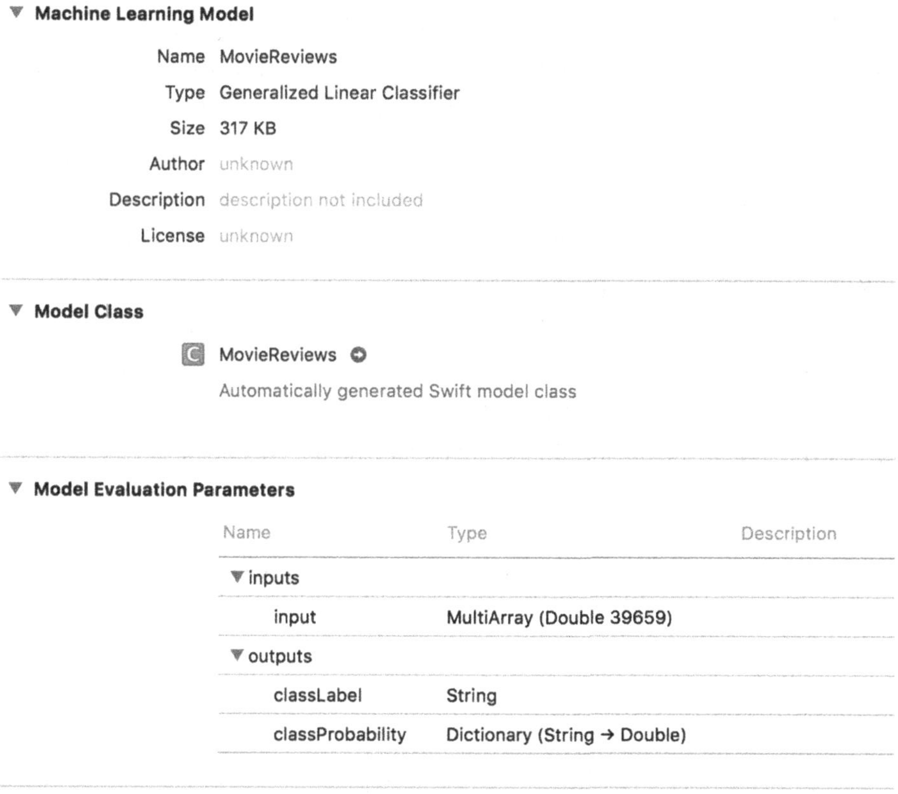

▼ **Machine Learning Model**

Name	MovieReviews
Type	Generalized Linear Classifier
Size	317 KB
Author	unknown
Description	description not included
License	unknown

▼ **Model Class**

[C] MovieReviews ○

Automatically generated Swift model class

▼ **Model Evaluation Parameters**

Name	Type	Description
▼ inputs		
input	MultiArray (Double 39659)	
▼ outputs		
classLabel	String	
classProbability	Dictionary (String → Double)	

Figure 7-2. Generated Core ML model for movie reviews

If you examine the movie review dataset and the words_ordered.txt file, you will see that it actually has 39,659 words. It is trained and tested with the TF-IDF vectorizer, so what you need here is to compute the TF-IDF weight factor for every word of the review the user has entered and put it at the exact place in MLMultiArray as it is ordered in the words_ordered.txt file. All the other entries in the multidimensional array (words that don't appear in the review) will be zeros, so they don't influence the result.

But now you have another big problem. You need to compute the TF-IDF weight, which requires word counts of all the occurrences of the words in the other 1,000 positive and 1,000 negative training reviews. If you do this every time the user types a review, you will put your users to sleep with your slowness and inefficiency. What you need is to precompute the word occurrences and the index in the word ordering for every word and put them in a dictionary so they can be accessed in real time, whenever they are needed. Precomputing will speed up the process a lot, and the resulting output is the words.json file (Listing 7-2). The JSON file has dictionary entries, where the key is the word from the review (movie in the sample). The value is the dictionary containing the values for the index of the word in the multidimensional array, as well as the count of the word in the training set.

Listing 7-2. JSON File with Precomputed Word Counts

```
{
    "movie" : { "index" : 123, "count" : 50 },
    ...
}
```

To do this, you will have to do more Python scripting. You go through all the text files in the positive and negative datasets and count each word in every file. You iterate through the ordered words array in words_ordered.txt to get the index of every word in the multidimensional array (Listing 7-3).

Listing 7-3. Precomputing Word Counts

```
import os
import re
import json
import sys

sys.stdout=open('words.json','w')
from collections import Counter
from glob import iglob
wordsRaw = open('words_ordered.txt', 'r')
words_array = []
for line in wordsRaw:
        words_array.append(line.rstrip())
frequency = {}

def removegarbage(text):
    text=re.sub(r'\W+',' ',text)
    text=text.lower()
    return text

folderpaths=['txt_sentoken/pos/', 'txt_sentoken/neg/']
counter=Counter()

for folderpath in folderpaths:
        for filepath in iglob(os.path.join(folderpath,'*.txt')):
                with open(filepath,'r') as filehandle:
                        counter.update(removegarbage
                        (filehandle.read()).split())

for word,count in counter.most_common():
        frequency[word] = count
result = {}
```

```
index = 0
for word in words_array:
        info = {}
        info["count"] = frequency[word]
        info["index"] = index
        result[word] = info
        index += 1
print(json.dumps(result))
```

Doing the iOS App Implementation

That's everything you need to get started with coding the iOS app, which is the simpler part in this case. Open the starter project for this chapter (with the Core ML model included), or create your own single-view application with the user interface provided in Figure 7-3 and call it SentimentAnalysis.

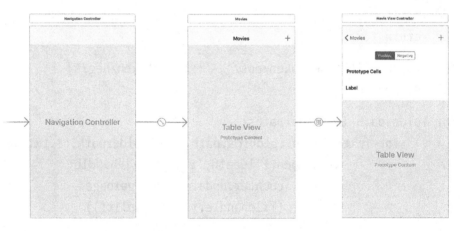

Figure 7-3. *User interface of the movie reviews app*

You will store the movies locally, in UserDefaults. For this app, you only need the title of the movie, as well as the positive and negative reviews for the movie. The MovieManager class takes care of this; it provides

196

methods for adding and listing movies, as well as adding and retrieving reviews for a particular movie (Listing 7-4).

Listing 7-4. Movie Manager Implementation

```
class MovieManager {

    private let moviesKey = "moviesKey"
    private let positivesKey = "positivesKey"
    private let negativesKey = "negativesKey"
    private var savedMovies = Dictionary<String,
    Dictionary<String, Array<String>>>()
    static let sharedInstance = MovieManager()

    init() {
        if let saved = UserDefaults.standard.value(forKey:
        moviesKey) {
            savedMovies = saved as! Dictionary<String,
            Dictionary<String, Array<String>>>
        }
    }

    func movies() -> Dictionary<String, Dictionary<String,
    Array<String>>> {
        return savedMovies
    }

    func addMovie(withTitle title:String) {
        let moviesInfo: Dictionary<String, Array<String>> =
        [positivesKey : [], negativesKey : []]
        savedMovies[title] = moviesInfo
        saveChanges()
    }

    func addReview(toMovieTitle movieTitle: String, review:
    String, sentiment: ReviewSentiment) {
```

```swift
        var key = positivesKey
        if sentiment == .Bad {
            key = negativesKey
        }
        if var movieInfo = savedMovies[movieTitle] {
            var reviews = [String]()
            reviews = movieInfo[key]!
            reviews.append(review)
            movieInfo[key] = reviews
            savedMovies[movieTitle] = movieInfo
        } else {
            var movieInfo: Dictionary<String, Array<String>> =
            [positivesKey : [], negativesKey : []]
            let reviews = [review]
            movieInfo[key] = reviews
            savedMovies[movieTitle] = movieInfo
        }
        saveChanges()
    }

    func positiveReviews(forMovieTitle movieTitle: String) ->
    [String] {
        return reviews(forMovieTitle: movieTitle, key:
        positivesKey)
    }

    func negativeReviews(forMovieTitle movieTitle: String) ->
    [String] {
        return reviews(forMovieTitle: movieTitle, key:
        negativesKey)
    }

    private func reviews(forMovieTitle movieTitle: String, key:
    String)
```

```
    -> [String] {
        if let movieInfo = savedMovies[movieTitle] {
            return movieInfo[key]!
        } else {
            return []
        }
    }

    private func saveChanges() {
        UserDefaults.standard.set(savedMovies, forKey:
        moviesKey)
        UserDefaults.standard.synchronize()
    }
}
```

The most interesting part here is the addReview(toMovieTitle, review, sentiment:) method. The method takes a movie title, a review, and a sentiment and saves them to your internal storage. For the sentiment, you define an enumeration since you don't want to work with plain strings (Listing 7-5).

Listing 7-5. Sentiment Enumeration in the MovieManager

```
enum ReviewSentiment {
    case Good
    case Bad
}
```

The movies stored in MovieManager are used as data sources in the initial ViewController that is shown on application start (Listing 7-6). The movies are presented in a table view. Whenever the user selects one of the listed movies, a new screen is shown that displays the positive and negative movie reviews.

Listing 7-6. Displaying Movies in a Table View in ViewController. swift

```
func tableView(_ tableView: UITableView,
                      numberOfRowsInSection section: Int) ->
                      Int {
        return MovieManager.sharedInstance.movies().count
}

func tableView(_ tableView: UITableView,
                      cellForRowAt indexPath: IndexPath) ->
                      UITableViewCell {
        var cell = tableView.dequeueReusableCell(withIdentifi
        er: cellIdentifier)
        if cell == nil {
            cell = UITableViewCell(style: .default,
            reuseIdentifier: cellIdentifier)
        }

        let movieTitle =
            Array(MovieManager.sharedInstance.movies().keys)
            [indexPath.row]
        cell?.textLabel?.text = movieTitle

        return cell!
}
```

As mentioned at the beginning of the chapter, the app will allow users to add movies they want to review. Both adding and reviewing of the movies will require a similar alert controller, with small modifications. To reuse the common functionality between these two features of the app, you define two helper methods in a new Swift file called Util.swift. The first one creates an alert controller with a title and an input field with a placeholder (Listing 7-7).

Listing 7-7. Creating an Alert for Adding Items in Util.swift

```
func alertForAddingItems(title: String,
                         placeholder: String)
-> UIAlertController {
    let alertController = UIAlertController(title: title,
                                            message: nil,
                                            preferredStyle:
                                            .alert)
    alertController.addTextField { textField in
        textField.placeholder = placeholder
    }

    return alertController
}
```

The second helper method adds to the created alert controller Save and Cancel buttons and an action that needs to be performed when the Save button is tapped (Listing 7-8).

Listing 7-8. Helper Method for Adding Save and Cancel Buttons to an Alert Controller, Defined in Util.swift

```
func addActions(toAlertController alertController:
UIAlertController,
                saveActionHandler: @escaping ((UIAlertAction)
                -> Swift.Void))
   -> UIAlertController {
      let saveAction = UIAlertAction(title: "Save",
                       style: .default,
                       handler: saveActionHandler)
      let cancelAction = UIAlertAction(title: "Cancel",
                                       style: .cancel,
                                       handler: { action in
```

```
                                        alertController.
                                        dismiss(animated:
                                        true,
                                        completion: nil)
                        })
    alertController.addAction(saveAction)
    alertController.addAction(cancelAction)
    return alertController
}
```

When the user taps the navigation bar button for adding movies in the ViewController, you use these two methods to display the pop-up for adding the movie. In the saveActionHandler, you call the MovieManager's addMovie(withTitle:) method to persist the movie locally on the user's device (Listing 7-9).

Listing 7-9. Alert for Adding Movies in ViewController.swift

```
private func alertForAddingItems() -> UIAlertController {
    let alertController = SentimentAnalysis.
    alertForAddingItems(
                        title: "Please provide movie
                        title",
                                placeholder: "Movie
                                title")
    return addActions(toAlertController: alertController,
                    saveActionHandler: { [unowned self]
                    action in
                        let textField = alertController.
                        textFields![0]
                        if let text = textField.text {
                            if text != "" {
                                MovieManager.
                                sharedInstance.addMovie(
```

```
                                    withTitle: text)
                                self.tableView.reloadData()
                        }
                }
                alertController.dismiss(animated:
                true, completion: nil)
        })
}
```

Then, you need to call this method when the user taps the add button, by implementing its @IBAction method in the ViewController (Listing 7-10). This presents the pop-up with a text field to the user.

Listing 7-10. Implementing the Click Handler of the Add Button

```
@IBAction func addButtonClicked(button: UIButton) {
        let alertController = self.alertForAddingItems()
        self.present(alertController, animated: true,
        completion: nil)
}
```

The last thing you need to do in the ViewController is to implement the selection of a movie from the table view, as well as pass the selected data to the next view controller, which is the MovieViewController (Listing 7-11). In the didSelectRow method of the table view, you just save the selection and perform the showMovieReviews segue. In the prepare method for the segue, you pass the movie title to the MovieViewController.

Listing 7-11. Selecting a Movie from the List

```
private var selectedIndex: IndexPath? // defined as var in the
ViewController

func tableView(_ tableView: UITableView,
```

```
            didSelectRowAt indexPath: IndexPath) {
        tableView.deselectRow(at: indexPath, animated: true)
        selectedIndex = indexPath
        performSegue(withIdentifier: "showMovieReviews",
        sender: self)
}

override func prepare(for segue: UIStoryboardSegue, sender:
Any?) {
        if segue.identifier == "showMovieReviews" {
            let movieTitle = Array(MovieManager.sharedInstance.
            movies().keys)[selectedIndex!.row]
            let next = segue.destination as!
            MovieViewController
            next.movieTitle = movieTitle
        }
}
```

Next, let's switch to the MovieViewController, which contains the
most interesting parts. In Listing 7-12, you define a few variables that are
needed in the implementation of this view controller.

Listing 7-12. MovieViewController Variables

```
private var currentSentiment: ReviewSentiment = .Good
private var wordCountings = Dictionary<String,
Dictionary<String, Int>>()
let movieReviews = MovieReviews()
var movieTitle: String!
```

The MovieViewController will display either the positive or negative
reviews based on the selection of a segmented control at the top of the
screen. The currentSentiment variable will keep track of the current state
of the segmented control. The variable wordCountings is used to store

the contents of the words.json file, which you generated in the previous section. This variable will help you in computing the TF-IDF value of the words in the movie review. The movieReviews constant holds the generated Core ML class, used for interacting with the model you have integrated into your project.

First, let's populate the wordCountings dictionary by calling the loadWordCountings method in the viewDidLoad method of the MovieViewController (Listing 7-13).

Listing 7-13. Loading the Counts of the Words

```
private func loadWordCountings() {
        let wordsUrl = Bundle.main.url(forResource: "words",
        withExtension: "json")!
        do {
            let wordsData = try Data.init(contentsOf: wordsUrl)
            wordCountings = try JSONSerialization.
            jsonObject(with: wordsData,
                            options: .allowFragments)
                as! Dictionary<String, Dictionary<String, Int>>
        } catch {
            print("error loading words")
        }
}
```

Next, you need to display the reviews that are already saved in the MovieManager. Based on the currentSentiment state, you load either the positive or the negative movie reviews in the table view of the MovieViewController (Listing 7-14).

Listing 7-14. Presenting the Movie Reviews in a Table View in the MovieViewController

```swift
func tableView(_ tableView: UITableView, numberOfRowsInSection
section: Int) -> Int {
        if currentSentiment == .Good {
            return MovieManager.sharedInstance.positiveReviews(
                forMovieTitle: movieTitle).count
        } else {
            return MovieManager.sharedInstance.negativeReviews(
                forMovieTitle: movieTitle).count
        }
}

func tableView(_ tableView: UITableView,
                cellForRowAt indexPath: IndexPath) ->
                UITableViewCell {
        let cell = tableView.dequeueReusableCell(
                withIdentifier: cellIdentifier) as! ReviewCell
        var review = ""
    if currentSentiment == .Good {
                review = MovieManager
                .sharedInstance
                .positiveReviews(forMovieTitle: movieTitle)
                [indexPath.row]
    } else {
            review = MovieManager
                .sharedInstance
                .negativeReviews(forMovieTitle: movieTitle)
                [indexPath.row]
    }
    cell.reviewLabel.text = review
    return cell
}
```

What follows is the implementation of adding the movie reviews. For this, you will reuse your two helper methods to create an alert controller with save functionality. In the `saveActionHandler` of `addActions(toAlertController:, saveActionHandler:)`, you read the entered value from the text field and then determine the sentiment of that value using the `MovieReviews` model. Afterward, you save the review, along with the sentiment, using the `MovieManager`'s `addReview(toMovieT itle:review:sentiment)` method (Listing 7-15). Add this method in the `MovieViewController`.

Listing 7-15. Alert for Adding Movie Reviews

```
private func alertForAddingItems() -> UIAlertController {
        let alertController = SentimentAnalysis.
        alertForAddingItems(
                                title: "Please give movie review",
                                    placeholder: "Movie
                                    review")
        return addActions(toAlertController: alertController,
                        saveActionHandler: { [unowned self]
                        action in
                          let textField = alertController.
                          textFields![0]
                          if let text = textField.text {
                              if text != "" {
                                  MovieManager.
                                  sharedInstance.addReview(
                                          toMovieTitle: self.
                                          movieTitle,
                                           review: text,
                                           sentiment: self.
                                           sentiment
                                           (forReview: text))
```

```
                              self.tableView.reloadData()
                    }
              }
              alertController.dismiss(animated:
              true, completion: nil)
    })
}
```

How do you determine the sentiment here? The
sentiment(forReview:) method does that. It receives string input
entered by the user, calls the convert(string:wordCountings) method
(which you will see in Listing 7-17), and then sends the newly created
multidimensional array to the MovieReviews Core ML model. The model
tries to make a prediction, and if it fails, you will be nice and assume it's a
positive review. If the prediction is successful, you check which polarity
has bigger class probability and use that as a sentiment (Listing 7-16).

Listing 7-16. Determining the Sentiment of a Movie Review

```
private func sentiment(forReview review: String) ->
ReviewSentiment {
        let mlMultiArray = SentimentAnalysis.convert(
                                    string: review,
                                    wordCountings:
                                    wordCountings)
        guard let predictionOutput = try? movieReviews.
        prediction(
                                    input: mlMultiArray)
else {
            print("Error producing sentiment, setting good
            sentiment as default")
            return .Good
        }
```

```
        return sentiment(forPrediction: predictionOutput)
    }

private func sentiment(forPrediction prediction:
MovieReviewsOutput)
-> ReviewSentiment {
        let goodSentiment = prediction.classProbability["good"]!
        let badSentiment = prediction.classProbability["bad"]!
        if goodSentiment > badSentiment {
            return .Good
        } else {
            return .Bad
        }
}
```

The convert(string:wordCountings) method takes the user review and the wordCountings value that you loaded from the words.json file as input and returns MLMultiArray with TF-IDF weight factors. You do this by creating MLMultiArray and filling everything with zeros. Then, you get the words from the sentence by removing the punctuation and whitespaces. You can also do this with NSLinguisticTagger (see the previous chapter for more details). Then you go through the separated words and try to get the word count and index from the precomputed dictionary wordCountings. You use this information to compute the TF-IDF factor and update the multidimensional array index with the new value (Listing 7-17). Add this method in the Util.swift file you created earlier.

Listing 7-17. Converting a String to Multidimensional Input for Core ML

```
func convert(string: String,
            wordCountings: Dictionary<String,
            Dictionary<String, Int>>)
```

```
-> MLMultiArray {
guard let mlMultiArray = try?
        MLMultiArray(shape:[NSNumber(integerLiteral:
        ArraySize)],
                        dataType:MLMultiArrayDataType.double)
    else {
        fatalError("Unexpected runtime error. MLMultiArray")
    }

    for i in 0..<ArraySize {
        mlMultiArray[i] = 0
    }

    let separatedWords: [String] = string
        .components(separatedBy: .punctuationCharacters)
        .joined()
        .components(separatedBy: .whitespaces)
        .filter{!$0.isEmpty}

    for word in separatedWords {
        if let wordInfo = wordCountings[word] {
            let index = wordInfo["index"]!
            let countInDoc = wordInfo["count"]!
            let wordOccurencies = occurencies(ofWord: word,
                                    inList: separatedWords)
            let tf =
                Double(wordOccurencies) / Double(separatedWords.
                count)
            let idf =
                log(Double(wordCountings.count) /
                Double(countInDoc))
            mlMultiArray[index] = NSNumber(value: tf * idf)
        }
    }
```

```
        return mlMultiArray
}

private func occurencies(ofWord word: String, inList list:
[String])
-> Int {
    var count = 0
    for entry in list {
        if entry == word {
            count += 1
        }
    }
    return count
}
```

Before you test the app, you need to add methods that handle a selection change of the segmented control, as well as the tap of the button for adding movie reviews (Listing 7-18).

Listing 7-18. Handling Segmented Control Selection Change and Add Button Tap

```
@IBAction func segmentedValueChanged(control:
UISegmentedControl) {
        if control.selectedSegmentIndex == 0 {
            currentSentiment = .Good
        } else {
            currentSentiment = .Bad
        }
        updateState()
}

private func updateState() {
        tableView.reloadData()
}
```

```
@IBAction func addButtonClicked(button: UIButton) {
        let alertController = self.alertForAddingItems()
        self.present(alertController, animated: true,
        completion: nil)
}
```

If you now try the app, add any movie (let's say *Harry Potter*), and
open the movie details, you can start adding reviews. Let's first try with few
positive ones, such as "Unique and amazing, one of the best movies ever."
You will see that your model will classify this review in the positive section,
along with other similar reviews such as "Excellent movie, I really enjoyed
watching it." This is what you were expecting (Figure 7-4).

Figure 7-4. *Adding a positive movie review*

Let's now add some negative reviews, such as "This movie sucks, it's weird and boring." The model will correctly classify this as a negative review (Figure 7-5).

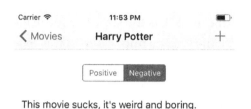

Figure 7-5. *Negative reviews*

Of course, sentiment analysis doesn't always work perfectly. Implementing machine learning and training a model are really hard to get right, and a margin of error is always present. If you try several different examples, you will see that it might produce a wrong sentiment sometimes.

Understanding Core ML Limitations

This leads us to the biggest problem of Core ML: the models can't be trained additionally after the user starts using the app. For example, if a review is classified in the wrong polarity, the user cannot provide input that this is the wrong answer. Therefore, the Core ML model won't be able to learn and improve for future similar requests. Core ML only makes predictions on previously trained models; it's not a machine learning framework itself. Let's hope that this will be enabled in future versions. One workaround would be to ask the user whether a prediction was correct and send that answer to your back end. When you have enough such corrections, you could retrain your model and submit an app update. It's not that elegant, but it can be used as a workaround until there is better way.

That also prevents you from providing a customized user experience. If you want to learn the preferences of users and based on that give recommendations (like, for example, in a music app), that's currently not possible with Core ML.

Another issue with Core ML is the size. The more test data you add, the bigger the model. This is not a huge issue in this example since you are dealing with text, but it might be when dealing with images or larger text datasets. No one would install an app bigger than 100 MB to 200 MB.

In any case, Core ML provides iOS software engineers with a great tool to get started with machine learning. The main role of Core ML currently is to bridge the gap between academics (who do the work of researching, designing algorithms, and training datasets) and developers (who don't have much machine learning expertise but know how to bring production-ready apps to the real world). The framework is still in its early phases, so it will improve a lot, as will your know-how of it and machine learning in general.

Summary

To sum up, you used the Core ML framework for sentiment analysis of movie reviews. You trained a model using the scikit-learn framework with an already available large dataset of movie reviews. You then used Apple's coremltools to convert the model to its proprietary Core ML model. After this model was integrated in Xcode, you generated an interface for accessing the model. You then computed the TF-IDF value for every new sentence and sent a multidimensional array with the inputs to the model. Core ML returned a prediction of whether a movie review was positive or negative. Based on this information, you saved the movie reviews locally and displayed them separately in a filtered list. The process is illustrated in Figure 7-6. The machine learning step is more suitable for a data scientist. Choosing the right dataset, implementing the right machine learning algorithm, and fine-tuning and changing the parameters requires a lot of expertise in this area. The second step, the iOS integration, is where developers step in. They can easily integrate the Core ML model and focus on what they do best, which is creating apps and utilizing the established mobile technologies and concepts.

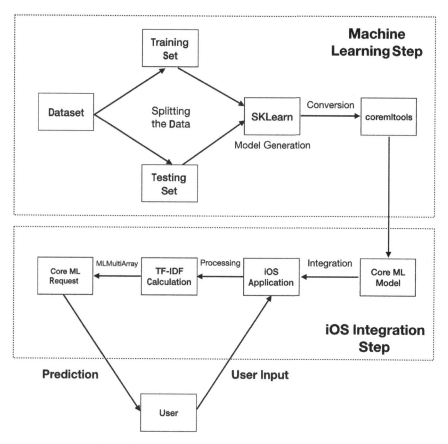

Figure 7-6. *Overview of the process of doing sentiment analysis with Core ML*

CHAPTER 8

Conversational Interface Challenges

In the previous chapters, you learned about the current state of conversational interfaces on a technical level. In this chapter, you'll see what challenges developers might face in this area and what you can expect in the future.

Security

Probably the biggest challenge is security. I mentioned in Chapter 1 how easy it is to give voice commands to mobile devices; it feels natural and in line with our interactions with people. However, someone else can come near your phone and say "Hey, Siri, send a million dollars to my account with number 123." If you were lucky enough to have that kind of money in your account, you would not have it anymore. The same applies to other domains that Siri supports. For example, there is the Car Commands domain. Someone else could say "Hey, Siri, unlock my car." If you are in a crowded place, you might not even hear this happen. Even worse, Siri can send messages on your behalf. Imagine someone else sending vicious messages to your loved ones from your phone just by giving a voice command or instructing the phone to call your boss at 4 a.m. Siri can also

© Martin Mitrevski 2018
M. Mitrevski, *Developing Conversational Interfaces for iOS*,
https://doi.org/10.1007/978-1-4842-3396-2_8

give access to your photo album, which contains private photos. As you can see, there are countless examples where security and privacy are big issues for Siri and other voice assistants.

How do you address this? The first and most obvious protection that comes to mind is to restrict the phone to accept commands only from your own voice. With Siri, you can already do that. If you go to Settings ➤ Siri, you will see a switch that says Allow "Hey Siri" that will guide you to a five-step training, after which Siri will respond only to your commands (Figure 8-1).

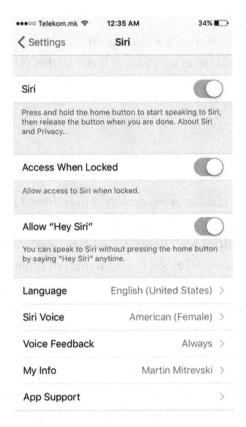

Figure 8-1. *Making Siri respond only to your voice*

However, a lot of users probably don't know about this feature and expose Siri to everyone. We, as developers, don't have information about whether a user has activated this protection, so you have to be careful about providing options via a voice interface. Another problem here might be if the user is recorded while speaking, someone could create a voice command by combining parts of the recording.

For the Speech framework, currently there is no such protection. It's probably not needed that much because the only way to use it is while the application is running in the foreground. If the unlocked phone is in bad hands, then both the touch interface and the voice commands are exposed at the same level, so the standard security issues for regular apps are applicable here as well.

The next level of protection is to provide authentication when sensitive data is requested. With Siri, in the Info.plist file of the extension, where you define extension attributes and which intents are supported, there is an additional key called IntentsRestrictedWhileLocked. Here, you can define the intents that require the user to unlock the phone before proceeding with the execution of the Siri request (Figure 8-2).

Key	Type	Value
▼ Information Property List	Dictionary	(10 items)
Localization native development r... ⌃	String	en
Bundle display name ⌃	String	RoutingSiri
Executable file ⌃	String	$(EXECUTABLE_NAME)
Bundle identifier ⌃	String	$(PRODUCT_BUNDLE_IDENTIFIER)
InfoDictionary version ⌃	String	6.0
Bundle name ⌃	String	$(PRODUCT_NAME)
Bundle OS Type code ⌃	String	XPC!
Bundle versions string, short ⌃	String	1.0
Bundle version ⌃	String	1
▼ NSExtension ⌃	Dictionary	(3 items)
▼ NSExtensionAttributes	Dictionary	(2 items)
▼ IntentsRestrictedWhileLocked	Array	(1 item)
Item 0	String	INRequestRideIntent
▼ IntentsSupported	Array	(2 items)
Item 0	String	INRequestRideIntent
Item 1	String	INGetRideStatusIntent
NSExtensionPointIdentifier	String	com.apple.intents-service
NSExtensionPrincipalClass	String	$(PRODUCT_MODULE_NAME).IntentHandler

Figure 8-2. *Setting restricted intents for Siri*

Additional protection can be added just before performing a sensitive action, such as sending money or unlocking a car. You can accomplish this both in Siri and in the Speech framework using the LocalAuthentication framework. This framework supports two forms of authentication: by entering a user's passcode and by using Touch ID (or Face ID if you have an iPhone X). Only after the users authenticate themselves can you proceed with the execution of the sensitive task. Listing 8-1 shows how you can ask for Touch ID or Face ID. Note that you don't have to specify which form of identification you need. The framework itself will determine, based on the device, which authentication will be presented. However, you as a developer should not use text (for localizedReason) that contains either the Touch ID or Face ID string since that might confuse users if they don't have that form of authentication.

Listing 8-1. Asking for Touch ID or Face ID

```
let context = LAContext()
var authError: NSError?
If context.canEvaluatePolicy(
                    LAPolicy.deviceOwnerAuthentication
                    WithBiometrics,
                    error: &authError) {
     context.evaluatePolicy(
                    LAPolicy.deviceOwnerAuthentication
                    WithBiometrics,
                    localizedReason: "Allow Siri to unlock
                    your car")
          { (success, evaluateError) in
             if (success) {
                // User authenticated successfully, perform
                action
             } else {
```

```
            // User did not authenticate, show an error
        }
    }
} else {
        // Could not evaluate policy; present a message to
        user
}
```

The user will be presented with the standard Touch ID pop-up (Figure 8-3). If your app executes payments, you can also use Apple Pay directly; you will get the authentication part for free.

Figure 8-3. *Siri Touch ID pop-up*

This works nicely, but it requires interaction with the phone, either by typing a four- or six-digit passcode or by providing your fingerprint. So, it's not conversational anymore. There are already biometric companies that try to tackle this, especially in the intersection of conversational interfaces and the Internet of Things. There probably isn't a perfect single solution;

it will be a combination of biometrics, such as voice, face, touch, eye, and palm. One cool approach is to analyze your movement and gestures over time by using the iPhone sensors to detect whether it is really you holding the phone. This, combined with additional voice confirmation like "My voice is my password," might be secure enough. It's a really interesting topic, and it will be exciting to see innovations in this area.

Quality

Although there are significant improvements in machine learning and natural language processing, there is still a lot of room for improvement. For example, in the speech detection part, words with similar pronunciation are often mixed up. If you want to say "eye," the speech recognition system might detect that as "I," or vice versa. There are a lot of examples like this, and the more you use conversational interfaces, the more you will see them. Such issues can't be solved completely, but getting an idea of the broader context of the conversation, or about the type of application that is using them, might improve the results.

Noise is also a problem. When you think of the typical user of voice assistants, you usually think about someone who's always in a rush, in crowded places, or driving while music is playing. All those sounds in the background can affect the quality of the recognized text and, in the end, can affect the ability to understand what the user is trying to say. In any case, addressing this issue would be one of the most critical success factors of conversational interfaces.

Project Common Voice

Another challenge in the quality of natural language understanding is the lack of voice data. No matter how sophisticated and advanced the algorithms are for intent detection and entities extraction, a key ingredient is the need for a large amount of testing data. However, most of the data collected by large companies is not available for everyone to use.

Mozilla has tried to address this issue by launching the project Common Voice. The project's goal is to open voice recognition to everyone. Through the web site (`https://voice.mozilla.org`), users can donate their voice by reading sample sentences (Figure 8-4). Also, users can validate whether other users have correctly read the sample sentences. This helps a lot in the voice recognition process.

Figure 8-4. Reading sentences for Mozilla's Common Voice project

The project is open source, with a Creative Commons License. Mozilla encourages developers to launch the same web site in multiple languages. With the project, Mozilla also tries to solve the problem with multilanguage support. Currently, only the most popular languages (particularly English) have good voice recognition and natural language understanding support. However, for conversational interfaces to obtain massive market adoption, there has to be good support in as many languages as possible. People will rarely use, for example, an English voice assistant when shopping in a country where English is not the native language. The community has the potential to provide enough data, and the Common Voice project is a step toward that goal.

Note   The Creative Commons License enables free distribution of a copyrighted work.

Is It Dangerous?

I mentioned the movie *Her* in Chapter 1. For those of you who haven't watched it, it's about a lonely writer who develops an unlikely relationship with an operating system. The operating system learns over time what the main character needs and adjusts itself based on that input. The writer becomes more and more dependent on the OS, losing touch with reality. This movie gives a glimpse of how dangerous artificial intelligence can be.

Such advancements in AI are not that far off. Dialogflow, which you explored in Chapter 4, has a Small Talk agent that offers lots of questions and phrases for you to answer. Based on that, it customizes its responses. In other words, it learns what you want to read or hear (Figure 8-5).

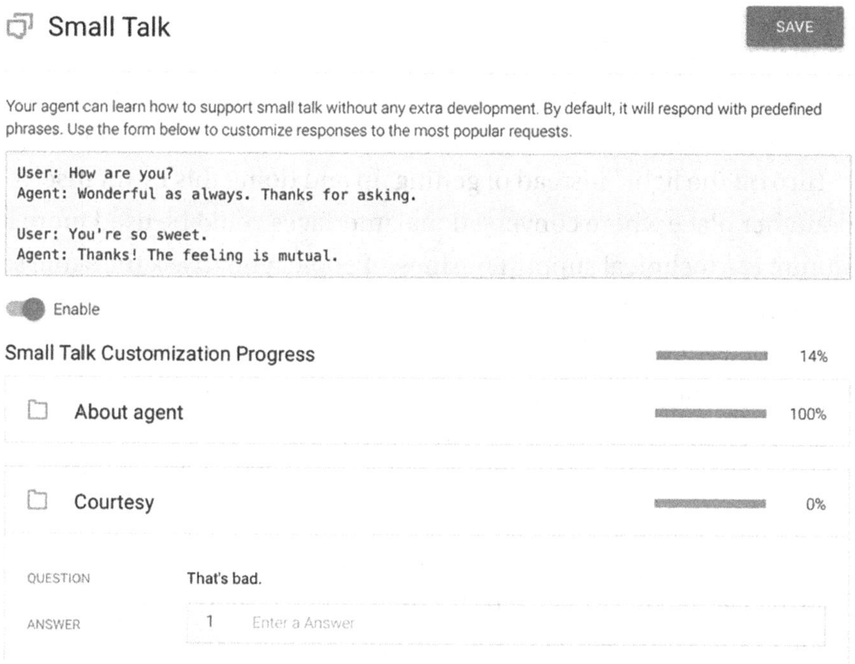

Figure 8-5. *Dialogflow's Small Talk agent*

Will People Use It?

That's the biggest question. Most people feel strange walking around the streets and talking with their voice assistants. A recent survey has shown that 98 percent have at least tried Siri, but only 3 percent of them have used it in public. The reason why they haven't used it in public is that they felt uncomfortable talking to their device in public. But when they are not surrounded by other people, such as when they are in a car or at home, people use voice assistants. Sixty-two percent of iPhone owners use Siri in the car, probably because they are less distracted by the phone and because of the hands-free driving laws.

Usage at home also makes sense since we are usually more comfortable at home (and lazier). With the rise of the smart home and the Internet of Things, conversational interfaces are needed more than ever. For example, if the light switch is far away from the bed, who wouldn't just say "Turn off the light" instead of getting up and doing this by themselves?

Another place where conversational interfaces could be used more in the future is a technical support business. People tend to ask the same set of questions when calling support people, which makes the introduction of a chatbot a good solution, at least as a filter for the standard questions. If the chatbots can't resolve the issue by themselves, the support people can take over. But then only a few support people would be needed, which brings us to the problem of artificial intelligence killing jobs—a topic worth an entire book.

These technologies can also be used in the service industries. Imagine people inspecting machines or trains or anything else that could be damaged and just saying "Oh, the window is broken here." Their assistant writes everything down and uploads it (along with the location) to the cloud. The repair person could see where the damage is and solve the problem with less communication and paperwork.

You have probably seen in a lot of movies the protocol that police officers following while investigating crimes. Detectives inspect the crime scene and look for details that will give indications about what happened. Everything they find is written in a report. Instead of typing everything, imagine the usage of voice assistants and natural language understanding. The detectives would just talk to their apps, which if trained with specific domain knowledge, would be able to categorize all the data into sections of a report, such as the location of the crime, clues, fingerprints found, and so on. It would help detectives save time by filling in the paperwork for them.

Training chatbots with domain knowledge and then using them as help in daily work is applicable to many other areas. For example, doctors could use such voice assistants while doing visits. They could ask the patients how are they feeling, and this information could be used to fill in a report generated by the voice assistant. Any other doctor notes, such as patient symptoms, condition updates, or questions, could also be directly included in the report.

Food businesses such as Subway use chatbots via Facebook Messenger already; the chatbots allow customers to order and pay for food without waiting in the line (Figure 8-6). Any service that has long queues of impatient people could use such technology.

Figure 8-6. *Subway Messenger chatbot for food ordering*

If you still have doubts about conversational interfaces, maybe this last example of the book will change your mind. Recently, a four-year-old child found his mom lying motionless in their home. With no one else around to help, the boy's last resort was the mom's phone nearby. He activated Siri, asked for help, and within 13 minutes the emergency service arrived, saving the mother's life. If there was no Siri, he probably wouldn't have been able to make the call. The phone was probably locked, and even if it was not, a four-year-old child probably wouldn't have known how to dial the emergency service number.

This highlights two great benefits of conversational interfaces: ease of use and accessibility. Even someone with modest technological knowledge is able to give commands that a machine will understand. This has the potential to make tech devices more accessible to everyone.

Summary

These are only few examples where conversational interfaces will be used in the future. As you can see, there are lots of opportunities and plenty of room for innovation. People might not use conversational interfaces in public yet, but for sure they will use them in contexts where they can get their jobs done more efficiently. The future of conversational interfaces is exciting. You can expect a lot of cool ideas, which will ideally make our lives easier and better.

Index

A, B

AVSpeechSynthesizer
  audioSession, 111, 121
  AVAudioSession, 122
  AVSpeechSynthesisVoice, 117
  AVSpeechUtterance, 111
  createRemainingText, 120
  createUtterance, 119–120
  LanguageViewController,
    114–115, 117–118
  navigation controller, grocery
    list storyboard, 114
  playRemainingText, 119
  saving, sliders' values, 116–117
  SettingsManager, 111–112, 116
  SettingsViewController,
    114–115
  setupSettingsButton, 121
  updating, recognition task,
    122, 124

C

Conversational interfaces
  benefits, 228
  Common Voice project,
    223–224
  crimes, movies, 226

Dialogflow's Small Talk agent,
  224–225
food businesses, 227
home usage, 226
quality, 222
security
  authentication, 219
  passcode/fingerprint, 221
  setting restricted intents for
    Siri, 219
  Speech framework, 219
  Touch ID or Face ID,
    220–221
  voice commands, 217–218
survey, 225
technical support business, 226
technologies, 226
training chatbots, 226

D, E, F

Dialogflow
  agent
    adding values, product
      entity, 126
    AddProduct intent, 127
    annotating entities, test
      sentences, 129

G, H, I, J, K

L

O, P, Q, R

S

Get the eBook for only $5!

Why limit yourself?

With most of our titles available in both PDF and ePUB format, you can access your content wherever and however you wish—on your PC, phone, tablet, or reader.

Since you've purchased this print book, we are happy to offer you the eBook for just $5.

To learn more, go to http://www.apress.com/companion or contact support@apress.com.

Apress®

Printed in the United States
By Bookmasters